PRAISE FOR *DIGITAL AGENCY FASTTRACK*

"One of the best books on business, marketing, and the business of marketing I have read. This books confirms Niel Malan as one of the leading internet marketing gurus in the world today. This book is about so much more than setting up a digital agency. It's so much more than Facebook or Google. It's about one of the greatest opportunities in the world today and how to leverage it to enable you and your clients to live a life of wealth and purpose."

–**Justin Cohen**
Bestselling Author, International Speaker

"I had the privilege of learning from Niel Malan by completing the Facebook Marketing Mastery and subsequently the Agency FastTrack Course. I have now also read his insightful and valuable *Digital Agency FastTrack* book and he has truly outdone himself! I am currently sitting next to the pool at my Bangkok hotel waiting for some friends to arrive so we can see in 2019. I have spent an hour this morning reviewing my client's digital campaigns and optimized it with the click of a few buttons on my laptop. I never would have thought I could do this and truly live the laptop lifestyle less than a year ago whilst being trapped in the corporate political rat race. Niel's book is a step-by-step recipe for becoming financially and (more importantly) time and corporate jail free! It is practical, to the point, and probably the most important book you will read in a very long time. Thank you Niel for showing me the way and affording me the opportunity to really live the laptop lifestyle! This is a MUST READ!!"

–**Brian Smith**
Digital Agency Owner, Agency FastTrack Graduate

"This book will open an incredible doorway to a new life for you! Just like Niel Malan has for me!!! This book outlines EVERYTHING you need to know about the Digital Marketing world! Giving you information on all the Technical side as well as Copywriting, Brand, and Advertising Strategies, Niel covers how to even find future Clients! I have read this book from cover to cover, and I'll probably read it again! I have done the Agency FastTrack Apprentice Program, and my Hair Salon Business has grown from Strength to Strength! I now have my own Agency helping other Salon Owners grow their businesses, and my time spent in my salon is now socializing with my clients and not breaking my back slogging behind the chair. I have never looked back and am eternally grateful to Niel Malan for landing up in his Facebook Funnel!"

–Candice Donadel
Digital Agency Owner, Salon Owner, Agency FastTrack Graduate

"What a great book! If you want to start a business that will give you financial and time freedom and to work from anywhere in the world then this is the book for you! I want to live the 'laptop lifestyle' and Niel makes me really believe it is possible! Very well written book full of information that would usually only be available from expensive courses or mentors. This is my new favourite book by far!"

–Chris Schoeman
Digital Agency Owner, Agency FastTrack Graduate

"Your book demonstrates your passion as an entrepreneur and business coach. What I loved about this book is that everything you describe is absolutely different yet completely doable. The passion of helping others to reach their dreams is self evident. Your content is factual and honest because of the practical approach taken to teach and guide students that are already enrolled in your Agency FastTrack course.

Your book is an inspiration to those who still dare to dream and who want more out of life. Thank you for sharing your knowledge with us so that we can continue to grow and reach new heights. To all those who want a new challenge and refuse to be one of the crowd I urge you to take the next step after reading the book. This is the prelude to your new opportunity of running a digital agency that is global. Many thanks."

–**Colleen Sharon Moyle**
Digital Agency Owner, Agency FastTrack Graduate

"If there is one must read book that will change your life, it is *Digital Agency FastTrack* by Niel Malan from Elite Inc.

This book will take you from novice to ninja in no time in the world of Digital Marketing. And what is more is that Niel does not only teach you all the necessary skills and brilliant digital marketing strategies up to the stage where you create your own digital agency, he teaches you the right values that makes an honest business successful. It's not about making money, that too, but in the first place it's about building a relationship with your client. It's about helping your client to get more paying customers to make more money and to build a better business for your client.

As I read through *Digital Agency FastTrack*, after every page I was more and more convinced that this book by Niel Malan will change your life! More financial freedom, more time to spend with your family, and you can work from anywhere in the world, as long as you have an internet connection.

His knowledge and expertise is superior, and what he writes about his Agency FastTrack Model is practical, understandable, and doable! If *Digital Agency FastTrack* can change my life, it can change yours."

–**Corneil Du Plessis**
Digital Agency Owner, Agency FastTrack Graduate

"The Guru of Facebook Marketing, Niel Malan has done it again! This time he shares all his secrets in a complete, refreshingly conversational, step by step guide. The easiest way ever to start your own digital marketing agency. Sick and tired of a rat race life? Begin your new chapter right here."

–Daleen Rodgers
Digital Agency Owner, Agency FastTrack Graduate

"An amazing, insightful, practical step by step guide and road map to achieve success. Niel Malan is a digital marketing master with an incredible understanding of business and the changing market environment. Highly recommend *Digital Agency FastTrack* to anyone looking for the right business opportunity / knowhow to achieve financial, location and time freedom. Take action now, I did, it changed my life. Thank you Niel and the entire team at Elite Inc."

–Gavin Powell
Digital Agency Owner, Agency FastTrack Graduate

"Niel Malan is not only a marketing genius, he is also a life coach. He has this amazing ability to just open your eyes to all those opportunities out there. This is not only game changing, this is LIFE changing. The content of his book speaks of many, many years of the vast knowledge he has built up. And he just loves to share it all!"

–Hans Ambulans
Digital Agency Owner, Agency FastTrack Graduate

"Easy to read, real and very practical advice! I really enjoyed reading this and it now has me super motivated to get back to work to start strategizing for 2019 - that on the 26th of December when I am supposed to be on holiday! This is also a great road-map and puts the Agency FastTrack program into perspective."

–Harry Meyburgh
Digital Agency Owner, Agency FastTrack Graduate

"Very easy to read, not boring, and packed with information. If you want to learn more about digital marketing, then this is a good place to start. Everything you need to know to start your own agency is discussed in here. I especially like the part about client onboarding and knowing what to look for in the ideal client. Highly recommend."

–Hendricus Vercueil
Digital Agency Owner, Agency FastTrack Graduate

"What a fantastic read! Packed with value and everything you need to get started on your journey of owning and running a successful digital agency. A must read if you are serious about getting started in the digital space!"

–Ilonka Lubbe-Ras
Digital Agency Owner, Agency FastTrack Graduate

"*Digital Agency FastTrack* has changed my life. I had the skills for digital marketing but was still stuck in a dead-end job, doing digital marketing as a hobby. Going through *Digital Agency FastTrack* has transformed my passion/hobby into my new profession. Niel is a master at explaining all the minor details and getting you off the ground in lightning speed.

What I LOVE about it, is that it's setup so anyone from any walk of life can understand it and follow along. TRULY LIFE CHANGING!!"

–Jacques Jaykita Rossouw
Digital Agency Owner, Agency FastTrack Graduate

"Niel Malan's *Digital Agency FastTrack* book is by far the best book I have read when it comes to all things Digital Marketing. This is my go to book from now on and it has helped me to take my own Digital Marketing Agency to the next level.

The way he brings his knowledge and teachings across is simple and straightforward. A complete beginner and the most experienced expert will get a lot out of the book. Anyone will be able to learn from it. He has so many practical examples and step by step instructions to follow that make learning these skills even easier.

Over and above the skills, there is so much added value that this book has given me. Not only did I learn about running a Digital Agency, but I learnt plenty of self development skills that I use on a daily basis. I am a better person just from reading this book. Thank you Niel Malan for pouring your heart out and giving us all of your secrets. I am forever grateful."

–Jason De Lange
Digital Agency Owner, Agency FastTrack Graduate

"I started reading Niel Malan's new book *Digital Agency FastTrack* last night, and that was a big mistake! It resulted in getting very little sleep...

Niel's passion and insight into the complete Digital Marketing industry is very inspirational and motivating. The book is an easy read, and it is clear from the very first page that if you are aspiring to become an expert (expert not guru) in the very relevant and current Digital Marketing Space, you are in the right place.

Today being the last day of 2018, I am filled with a wonderful expectation for 2019. Having Niel's book as part of my arsenal to guide me in growing my Digital Agency, I know that 2019 will be the year that counts."

–Kobus Bosman
Digital Agency Owner, Agency FastTrack Graduate

"I've known Niel Malan for more than ten years now. *Digital Agency FastTrack* is the fourth product I've purchased from him. With every product, Niel Malan has surpassed my expectation in terms of value for money. I trust Niel Malan and can recommend him and his products to new prospects. The book is truly a treasure trove of information about digital marketing."

–Lofty Fourie
Digital Agency Owner, Agency FastTrack Graduate

"Niel Malan is a genius and guru in the digital marketing world. This book got me all excited to start my own agency! In the book you will learn all the in's and out's of how to know what a successful digital marketer is supposed to do for your business and why you cannot afford not to use the services of one of his students to help your business grow.

Niel explains the concepts and ideas around digital marketing and the tools and techniques one has to master in layman's terms that makes it easy to digest and understand. A must read book for any small business owner wanting to grow and any person interested in learning the tools of the digital marketing trade. Ten out of ten."

–Lourens Van der Westhuizen
Digital Agency Owner, Agency FastTrack Graduate

"I loved the step by step structure of the book. I just found too many of what the other agencies do wrong (my mindset of rather focus on what I do best than what the competition do wrong). Great book. Definitely worth buying and using in conjunction with the Agency FastTrack program. After reading the book, you want to buy the program."

–Mandy McFarlane
Digital Agency Owner, Agency FastTrack Graduate

"Being a complete novice with regards to this whole new world with creating a digital agency, I have found that this book was very clear and concise in helping understand the gap in the market for experienced digital marketers. Being a current Agency FastTrack Student, reading this book has helped a lot to put things in context."

–Natalie Cassar
Digital Agency Owner, Agency FastTrack Graduate

"As usual Niel Malan over delivers on value. The book not only provides the 'Why?' for starting a Digital Marketing Agency, but also goes into a lot of detail about the all important 'How?'. After reading this book, I now know I am on the right track to achieve my dreams."

–Quinton Jacobs
Digital Agency Owner, Agency FastTrack Graduate

"It is only Niel Malan that can motivate his students to read his book before the year ends...so yes, I did read it, and I am very thankful that we are finished with the AFT course because everything that's in the book we learned during the past sixteen weeks...so yes, after reading that, I had a quick recap on the course and everything that is so important is just highlighted! Great book, something to keep nearby in our daily hustle doing what Niel said!"

–Riatha Eloff
Digital Agency Owner, Agency FastTrack Graduate

"Wow, what a powerful book. So relevant in this current time. Niel Malan, an expert in his own right, unpacks the opportunity to start your own digital agency and shares some critical knowledge that you require to have in order to run a successful high ROI digital agency.

Niel Malan, the man knows what he's talking about and has taught many of his students how to produce this High ROI digital agency he refers to in this book. Some of the points he breaks down amazing are the messaging that goes out to your SMB prospects, strategy, funnel building, understanding your ideal client. Oh, and lastly having that mindset of a business owner vs a self employed person. He continuous to breaks down going after the buck vs the mouse because this is where real money's at and how to position yourself to get these clients.

Brilliant book. Must read if you want to start a digital agency and are looking for a great business opportunity. This book is an intro of this powerful course, Agency FastTrack, where he teaches you to find high value clients, understand their business, develop a strategy, develop a funnel that converts, runnin Facebook ads, Google ads and then SCALE the business UP! No better place to learn than from the man who is actually doing it, Niel Malan."

–Ricardo Van Rooi
Digital Agency Owner, Agency FastTrack Graduate

"Niel is an incredibly smart guy who has developed an intensive understanding of human psychology, human nature, how we act and what provokes us. He has combined this all in becoming one of the best salesmen that I have come across. Taking this knowledge from an array of resources, he holds nothing back when it comes to selling and equally nothing back when it comes to sharing this vast knowledge. In his book, Niel encapsulates the digital marketing world and the requirements of owning and running a successful digital agency.

Sure, there is an overwhelming amount of information freely floating around the digital platform, but Niel transforms this information into knowledge, and I personally tend to disregard the noise out there if Niel has not recommended it through his material. Niel's hands-on attitude, which through his teaching is reflected by all of the Elite Inc. crew, is strongly conveyed through this book and his other resources."

–Rob Bower
Digital Agency Owner, Agency FastTrack Graduate

"Good easy to read book. Topics and information flow easily. I could not put the book down once I started! Informative provided TONS of excellent ideas and strategy for your agency or business. A must have in your list of readings."

–Ronelle Jacobsen
Digital Agency Owner, Agency FastTrack Graduate

"Niel's book explains very well why creating your agency is such a huge opportunity. It contains a wealth of knowledge and experience and actually guides you step by step from knowing nothing to the actual thought of selling your agency one day! The key to success is strategy, and Niel knows a lot about it!"

–Simeon Eloff

Digital Agency Owner, Agency FastTrack Graduate

"Excellent read! Gives detailed info on how to get started with your business and strive for financial freedom on your terms."

–Sophia Liu

Digital Agency Owner, Agency FastTrack Graduate

"What an amazing read. Niel has the ability to change the way you think about business."

–Stephan Kruger

Digital Agency Owner, Agency FastTrack Graduate

"Niel Malan's book, *Digital Agency FastTrack: Start, Build, and Scale a Seven-Figure Digital Agency* is what I would call a complete blueprint with expert information on how to start, create and run your successful online Digital Agency business.

Niel explains the twelve common mistakes the most of our newbie Online Marketer entrepreneurs make. I understand now what I have been doing wrong and how to fix it. Learn from the experts and save yourself TIME and MONEY.

It gives you information on how to create your successful online Digital Agency business. It explains with step by step detail and advice on how to determine who your target audience is and how to find them, attract them, and communicate with them.

With specialized knowledge and training, you can turn your business into a booming successful online Digital Agency. *Digital Agency*

FastTrack: Start, Build, and Scale a Seven-Figure Digital Agency is a must read book for any entrepreneur who wants to start their own online Digital Agency."

–Theuns Bester
Digital Agency Owner, Agency FastTrack Graduate

"Thank you Niel for such an inspiring book. If you want more feet through your doors or want to start an agency, this is a must read. Clear and so simple, even I can follow the blueprint. I will have this book on my desk for many years to come."

–Trevor Floyd
Digital Agency Owner, Agency FastTrack Graduate

"VERY useful book!!! As an existing agency owner, this book opened my eyes. There were many things that I did wrong and did not even know it was wrong. The impact on my agency was HUGE!"

–Willie Koen
Digital Agency Owner, Agency FastTrack Graduate

**DIGITAL AGENCY
FASTTRACK**

DIGITAL AGENCY FASTTRACK

START, BUILD, AND SCALE A SEVEN-FIGURE DIGITAL AGENCY

BY NIEL MALAN

Digital Agency FastTrack: Start, Build, and Scale a Seven-Figure Digital Agency Copyright © 2019 by Niel Malan

All rights reserved. No part of this publication may be reproduced, distributed, or transmitted in any form or by any means, including photocopying, recording, or other electronic or mechanical methods, without the prior written permission of the publisher, except in the case of brief quotations embodied in critical reviews and certain other noncommercial uses permitted by copyright law.

ISBN: 9781794114654 (paperback)

Imprint: Independently published

Printed in the United States of America

This publication is designed to provide accurate and authoritative information with regard to the subject matter covered. It is sold with the understanding that neither the author nor publisher is engaged in rendering legal, accounting, or other professional advice. If legal advice or other expert assistance is required, the services of a competent professional person should be sought.

CONTENTS

Chapter 1
The Opportunity of Your Lifetime 1

Chapter 2
The 12 Mistakes Every Newbie Makes (That You Don't Have To) 11

Chapter 3
Your High ROI Business Model. 23

Chapter 4
Your First High ROI Strategy: Audiences 29

Chapter 5
Your Second High ROI Strategy: Messaging 41

Chapter 6
Your Third High ROI Strategy: Funnels 59

Chapter 7
Marketing the Marketer: Finding Clients for Your Agency 67

Chapter 8
Buck Or Mouse? Vetting Your Clients 79

Chapter 9
Close the Deal: Sales, Pricing, and Onboarding 87

Chapter 10
Scaling For the Future: The Secret to Explode Your Agency's Profits . 99

Chapter 11
Built to Sell: Achieving the Ultimate Payday 107

Chapter 12
What's Next? Take A.C.T.ion. 119

Notes 129

CHAPTER 1

THE OPPORTUNITY OF YOUR LIFETIME

Have you ever thought about running your own business? Becoming an entrepreneur?

Living "the dream"?

If so, I have good news!

...and bad news.

First, the good news: It's easier than ever to make it on your own without a nine-to-five job. The Internet is a truly level playing field where the best idea, the best product, the best entrepreneur wins. If you have a Wifi connection, you can compete with million-dollar brands, whether you work from your local Starbucks or the beach.

Now, the bad news: When it comes to starting your own business, you may not have a choice. Nearly half of all people work for themselves, but not because entrepreneurship is everybody's Plan A.[1] These days, university degrees offer fewer and fewer career opportunities as more and more people graduate. Wages are stagnant across many different industries, and corporate ladders are shorter than ever.

Now, maybe none of this is actually news to you. After all, you picked up this book because you're looking for a positive change in your life. The idea of having your own business, setting your own hours, and working from the kitchen table (or wherever) seems *awesome*. But you're looking for something fresh, something new, something cutting edge...not tired, old concepts.

Over the last two decades, while coaching 100,000 business owners around the world, I have seen tens of thousands of aspiring entrepreneurs start a new business, only to close up shop within a few years.

Businesses that send their owner back into traditional employment with their tail tucked between their legs fail for a variety of reasons. Maybe the owner picked a cheap commodity product to sell, like plastic bracelets or information products. Or they tried to compete in a wickedly crowded industry like life coaching. Or worse, they started a business in a fading niche, like affiliate marketing, where the glory days are running out fast.

Of all these mistakes, that last one is the worst—trying to force your way through the window of opportunity after it's closed. Many business owners who attend my seminars tell me, "I'm struggling to grow my business. What have I been doing wrong?" Most of the time, they've been doing everything right, and the business itself isn't the problem. It's their industry; it's become stale.

If you want to succeed in a new business, especially in an online business, you need to follow the *right* opportunity at the *right time*. There's a million different things that can make you money online, but a lot of them are seasonal; they come and go, reappear again, and only last for a while. Search Engine Optimization (SEO) and generic web development each had a gravy train period, but it's come and gone. These services have become commoditized and no longer fetch the high premiums they used to.

That's why the best time to start a business is at the very *beginning* of a new trend. You want to discover gold in California in 1847, the year *before* the gold rush. You don't want to be the guy who shows up after the area is saturated with prospectors and merchants. And in business, you don't want to pursue an opportunity *after* all the money has been made.

To identify a business idea worth pursuing, **look for two specific things: high demand for the offer** and **a shortage of skills** you can easily acquire to meet that demand. Let's have a deeper look at both.

First, choose an industry in high demand. A lot of businesses fail because they start with a good business idea, but the concept itself is untested. Take the electric mouse trap. It seemed like a great product, but nobody wanted it.

The value of any product or service comes down to marketplace demand more so than how "good" a business idea is or how hard the owner works. There is little relationship between hard work and earnings. If there were, night shift construction workers would earn more than CEOs! But if the market says that a construction worker's labor is worth a certain amount, don't expect to earn much more if you show up at the job site with a hard hat.

The same applies to any skill set. You want to learn a high-paying skill that is going to be in high demand for years to come. Like Wayne Gretzky said, don't skate to where the puck *is*, skate to where the puck *is going*.[2]

Second, choose a high demand industry with a skills shortage, not a skills saturation. Let's say I want to hire a web marketing expert. I could probably find a million people to build a website and create social media content. Yes, the demand exists, but more people have the skill than need the skill. If you set up a generic web development agency in the late 1990s, you would have done incredibly well. Not so much today!

Another facet of high demand skills is how easy they are to acquire. If it takes four years and hundreds of thousands of dollars—like becoming a doctor—your opportunity may be gone by the time you're ready. In the online world, the cycle from opportunity to saturation can be very short.

If you find that sweet spot, you've got to move fast and commit yourself. There's a small window for you to get in and get market share before everyone else does. So don't take for granted how few opportunities there are that meet both criteria—huge demand *and* a skills shortage.

Right now, there is only *one* high demand, high-paying skill which is relatively easy to learn, even for people with no previous experience—**the skill of generating measurable return on investment (ROI) through focused digital marketing campaigns.**

The idea is very, very simple. Let's say a client pays you a hundred bucks, and you generate *three* hundred bucks for them in return. Chances are, you've just gotten yourself a paying client for life. The demand for somebody who knows how to create ROI will *never* go away, making it perhaps the number one most valuable skill in the digital age. People will always pay money to make money, and businesses—not individuals, not charities, not governments, but *businesses*—have the upfront money to afford to pay for it. You may run out of customers to keep your online bracelet store in business, but you will never run out of clients if you can produce a sustainable, measurable return on investment.

So, how do you turn one hundred dollars into three hundred...or three thousand? How do you do it *online*? And how do you know it's an in-demand, high-paying skill that *you* should learn?

Those questions are why I wrote this book. If you're playing the online business game for the first time, you are on the precipice of a very, *very* exciting opportunity. If you develop the requisite skill—generating ROI—to seize this opportunity, nothing is stopping you from earning $3,000, $5,000, even $10,000 per month and beyond. The best part is, this income is *sustainable*. Your clients love you, they stick with you, and you never have to worry about giving up and slogging back to a regular job.

I'm talking about having your very own **digital agency**. This is where *skill* and *opportunity* converge. As a digital agency owner, your job is to **strategize, launch, and manage advertising campaigns for businesses** on online platforms like Facebook and Google to **ultimately generate return on your clients' investment**.

There's a good reason why a digital agency is the best opportunity to make money online. Several reasons, actually! (Remember, you want to go into a growth-oriented industry where you're catching the wave, not chasing it.)

Reason number one: Small to medium sized businesses (SMBs) have been increasing their marketing and advertising budgets, and there is no sign of that slowing down anytime soon.

Some seventy percent of SMB owners say their digital marketing budgets will increase this year, with thirty percent of all owners increasing their budgets "considerably."[3] Regarding specific platforms, fifty-nine percent of business owners say they will increase marketing spending on social networks such as Facebook. That's why social media marketing spending is predicted to increase by a whopping ninety percent over the next five years.[4]

But just because a business *intends* to advertise more doesn't necessarily mean they'll actually get around to it. And if they do, there's very little chance of them doing it *well*. After all, the owner has a business to run!

Reason number two: SMBs *want* to advertise more, and they desperately need to, but they often don't follow through because they lack the time and the knowhow to spend their dollars wisely.

Right now, your future clients—SMBs—are facing a crisis. They look into the future, and they don't know if their business is in it. Everything from robots and software to outsourcing and ecommerce are picking off mom and pop shops left and right. The ones who've survived the rise of Walmart, Amazon, and other dominant businesses are barely hanging on.

To make matters worse, sales are becoming more and more inconsistent. Small businesses go through thriving cycles, where they can't keep up with business for three months out of the year. Then they go through four or five months of famine. The traditional marketing small business owners once relied on to dig themselves out of these revenue slumps doesn't work anymore, and they don't have time to learn anything new.

For example, one of my friends used to market her business at trade shows. For years, she turned a nice profit, but all of a sudden, trade show attendee numbers plummeted, and she lost thousands.

I know her pain. I used to take out double page ads in magazines to promote my business coaching services. For every $1,500 I spent, I'd make $13,000. Quite a bargain! But every year I renewed the ad, my returns went down while ad costs rose.

Traditional marketing, whether trade shows or print ads, is too much of a gamble. Business owners put money in a slot machine and have no guarantee anything's going to come out. They *know* they need to market—and they want to—but the risk is so damn high! They cannot afford to invest in marketing unless the results are predictable. Raising millions of dollars works great for a tech startup in Silicon Valley, but if you have a store, staff, and bills to pay, then one or two bad months wipe out the previous year's profits.

Meanwhile, internet marketing is a black hole. We know from reason number one that small business owners are setting aside whatever they can to invest in marketing in hopes of finding new customers, but ninety-nine percent of them are clueless about how social media and digital marketing work. I know this because I've not only talked with thousands of business owners over the last eighteen years, I've spied on their spending habits.

Don't take my word for it. According to Facebook Business Manager, of the approximately twenty million small businesses in the United States, fewer than **nine million** have a Facebook Page. But narrow down that number to include *only* SMBs that have spent money on digital advertising in the last ninety days, and that number drops to barely **110,000 businesses**. That means ninety-nine percent of US-based businesses need internet marketing help. They're not going to do it themselves, so just as they hire accountants for bookkeeping help, over eight million small businesses in the US alone are going to hire a digital agency (like the one I'm going to teach you how to build). I can't think of ANY business idea, opportunity, or trend this big!

Obviously, there is **demand** for digital agencies, but what about skills saturation? Don't thousands of agencies *already* exist to serve these businesses? This is where the opportunity for you to make a living becomes an opportunity to make a *fortune*. Yes, other agencies exist, but no, they don't have the skills. Welcome to **reason number three** to seize the digital agency opportunity: just like small business owners, the vast majority of agencies don't have a clue how to market and sell online!

It's just sad, really. A digital agency has one job to do: multiply clients' money through ROI-generating internet marketing. But most of them are so inept they can't even advertise their own businesses properly, much less their clients' businesses. For example, one of the simplest advertising tools in a digital agency's toolbox is called a **Tracking Pixel**, which is a short snippet of code on a website to track all new visitors. The Pixel "follows" these visitors to other platforms like Facebook so the business can market to them over and over until they buy. Simple, right?

Not so much. Of the top ten search results for "marketing agencies USA," a mere fifty percent have a website Tracking Pixel.

FIFTY PERCENT.

If digital agencies fail digital advertising 101 so badly right in front of our eyes, just think how poorly they're meeting demand and serving their clients.

This isn't rocket science. Do a Google search for a common small business in a big city, like "NYC dentists." Download a free browser extension like **Pixel Helper** to check the top *paid* search results. These businesses' websites receive *thousands* of hits per week, if not per day, from the Google Ads campaigns that some agency runs for them. But how many of the dentists' websites have a Tracking Pixel? I'm serious. Take a guess.

The week before I published this book, *none* of the top paid results for "NYC dentists" had a Tracking Pixel.

NONE.

Try this activity for "Los Angeles plumbers," "Miami optometrists," or "Chicago pizzerias," and you'll find the exact same problem. SMBs pay agencies thousands of dollars to turn new website visitors into new customers, but the agencies lack advertising knowhow, too!

Just imagine how much ROI these businesses could receive from a digital agency owner like you—somebody with the right skillset, somebody who knows how to generate ROI, *somebody who knows how to install a Tracking Pixel!*

If you seize the digital agency opportunity, you can become *more* than just another internet marketer (of which there are already too many!). As you generate leads and customers in every campaign, your clients will view you as **a long-term growth partner**. In return for meeting just a tiny fraction of the demand for ROI-generating online advertising services, you'll own a sustainable business with low churn and high value beyond your own skills.

If you ever want to sell your digital agency one day, *you can*! In 2016 alone, buying digital agencies was a four *billion*-dollar business.[5]

The selling price of most agencies is between eight and twelve *times* its annual profit,[6] and with **zero** overhead besides your laptop and Wifi, you are set for quite a payday.

With financial independence comes **location independence**, another great perk for digital agency owners. A sustainable business offers a sustainable lifestyle where you can jet set around the world, visiting a new country every two to three months, or spend more time with your family on your schedule, *not* your employer's. As long as you have your laptop and an internet connection, your clients couldn't care less where you are.

Location and income independence doesn't come without hard work, but owning a digital agency makes "the dream" doable. Having financial security while satisfying your travel bug is, well, *priceless*.

It's practical, too. In this day and age, the world is unpredictable. The water supply runs dangerously low in many coastal cities, terrorist attacks send people fleeing from their homelands, and stock markets rise and fall without warning. So if you can *live* anywhere because you can *work* anywhere, then you've got a **disaster-proof business**, my friend.

But the skills bar for this opportunity is very, very high. Small business owners expect return on their investment, not "promising results," not "increased engagement," and not "more hits." *Return on investment.* If you can't multiply a client's money, you won't see them sticking with you for more than two or three months. No business survives with that kind of turnover.

I've seen so many people's eyes light up when they realize how massive the digital agency opportunity is. They think, *As many as ninety-nine percent of small businesses are my future clients? Wow,* then they go mad. They buy a domain name, create a logo, and call themselves an agency. Three months later, every single client fires them, and they're back to selling bracelets.

Don't be that guy. Get the skills to generate ROI *first*. Get the advertising knowhow *first*. *Then* launch your digital agency. I promise you, you'll be glad you followed the right steps in the right order. Dozens of students have gone before you, and their successful businesses are a testament to a very simple fact—*this works*.

Yes, there's a lot to learn, but this book will teach you everything you need to know: how to seize the digital agency opportunity, how to create high ROI campaigns for small businesses, how to grow and run your very own agency, and much, much more. People just like you have built sustainable digital agencies with real-life paying clients, all from scratch, following the proven process outlined in this book. So if you're ready to learn, I'm ready to teach.

Ready?

CHAPTER 2

THE 12 MISTAKES EVERY NEWBIE MAKES (THAT YOU DON'T HAVE TO)

E ver heard of George Harrison?
  No, I'm not talking about *The Beatles* lead guitarist, I mean George Harrison the Australian mineral prospector. After the Dutch arrived at the tip of Southern Africa, rumors of an African El Dorado—The City of Gold—made their way back to Europe and all across the British Empire, beckoning adventurers and explorers to seek fortune beyond their wildest dreams.

One of the guys who listened was George Harrison. In the summer of 1886, George was on a typical morning stroll across a farm called *Langlaagte*. Exposed rock reflected sunlight, catching his eye. Plain sedimentary rock doesn't usually do that, so he looked closer.

Gold.

A hell of a lot of it. Within hours, George sent word to South Africa's then-government, who officially acknowledged his claim on the land. George Harrison had found El Dorado; the world's greatest gold rush began. With prospectors and entrepreneurs sailing to South Africa from California, England, and Australia all hoping to become "Randlords," old George did the last thing you'd expect.

He sold the farm.

No, George didn't sell the farm for a hefty profit. And he didn't sell the mining rights but keep the land. The guy didn't even bother recovering the bloody gold he'd spotted with his own eyes!

As the story goes, George Harrison sold his golden discovery for ten British pounds, about $1,700 in today's currency, and was never seen or heard from again. You read that right—**George Harrison sold El Dorado for the price of a used car.**

Do I have to say it? George Harrison was incredibly stupid. He stood at the tip of his continent's greatest opportunity, and he made a mistake that cost him his weight in gold probably ten thousand times over. From the South African Gold Rush, George walked away with a few bucks in his pockets while others walked away with millions. No one knows why he did what he did.

I can't tell you how many George Harrisons I've met in the digital agency world in the last few years. Both online and in person, I've shown people how ninety-nine percent of the small business market is untapped. It's unmined gold just sitting there for the taking.

Then for months, radio silence. When I follow up with these aspiring agency owners, I hear news I kind of expected: they started an agency, closed the agency, and moved on to the next shiny new thing.

Every time I ask why they gave up and left the industry completely, I hear one of about ten different excuses, all smoke screens. Behind each failure-justifying excuse is a beginner mistake that rips the golden agency opportunity from anyone's fingers before they know what the hell happened.

If your heart is set on seizing this opportunity, capitalizing on the online marketing trend, and starting a prosperous digital agency, learn from others' mistakes. In fact, I want you to learn how NOT to make these devastating mistakes <u>before you learn anything else</u>.

In other words, I won't let you sell a farm when there is gold all over the place. So let's protect your chances of success from the **Top Twelve Digital Agency Beginner Mistakes**.

CHAPTER 2 - THE 12 MISTAKES EVERY NEWBIE MAKES (THAT YOU DON'T HAVE TO)

Mistake number one: agency "experts" who don't actually run agencies.

Digital agency success is very, very difficult. That's why many people who expected to get rich quick got into the digital agency game, worked with two or three clients for a few months, and quit. Then their aspirations take them to another business model—creating online self-study courses. And they know barely enough about Facebook ads and Google PPC to be dangerous.

Have you seen these guys advertise their "courses"? Every single one of these agency "experts" sells their programs the same way—they create a free Facebook group, post a ton of contract screenshots "proving" how much their students make by following their program, and promise to help you launch your agency in thirty days or less. The dirty downside is that most of those $1500 per month clients in those screenshots fire the agency owner a few weeks into the contract. Any ambitious fool can trick a business owner to part with money once, but they don't have the requisite skills to offer return on their investment. One month of $1500 down the drain, and they're toast.

You don't want to be a one-hit wonder. Joining a program run by someone who doesn't actually operate their agency will make you exactly that. These one-trick pony programs exploit the need for instant gratification. Be very cautious about anyone who promises you'll get your first clients in a matter of weeks. They also all but guarantee riches from specific niches. Some programs give you a pre-built Funnel with all the copy, images, and videos targeting a certain profession like chiropractors or physical therapists. Congratulations—you're now one of about nine thousand people targeting the same businesses with identical advertisements!

If you do decide to join a program to expand and grow your digital agency skillset, choose mentors who enable you to succeed sustainably. For example, me and my team at Elite Inc. developed Agency FastTrack as an apprenticeship program. We're in the business of launching successful agencies run by people with the skills to grow them, scale them, and even sell them.

Instead of a hands-off program, we start by building a close bond between students, instructors, and support staff during a live in-person workshop. Over the course of four months, we "drip" one lesson at a time each week and hold all students accountable to learn and practice the material in the real world. An entire team works behind the scenes updating every lesson as technology changes—or goes obsolete.

We care whether or not people complete the program. The one man bands out there promising you the world only care that you join their course, keep a reliable credit card on file for your monthly payments, and leave them the hell alone. Agency FastTrack assigns each student a coach for moral support if you get frustrated while you're learning, and strategists for Funnel technical support. Anyone can tell you to, "Just press this button and launch your campaign, easy!" but that's rubbish. If you're new to digital marketing, tech problems murder you. Need help with your first funnel? Want to blow your first client's mind with ads that convert like mad? You've got around-the-clock technical support agents in Agency FastTrack who will take control of your computer remotely and show you how to fix your mistakes—right on your own screen.

Throughout your apprenticeship, you're under the tutelage of true experts who actually own digital agencies of their own. As you build your technical skill set and close your first clients, you're guided every step of the way to ensure your business survives—and thrives.

Mistake number two: free (mis)information.

"Why would I pay money for something I can get for free?" That's the excuse people give before they drown in free tutorial research results. Let me tell you a secret about the creators of those free videos on Facebook and Google advertising, digital marketing strategies, and funnel building tutorials. These people lock themselves in a room for a week, record the videos, and six months later, everything is out of date. But what do they care? A lot of these guys hype up the software they're showing you so you'll click their affiliate link and buy a license. They're the internet equals of used automobile salesmen.

Besides, why would you trust people who give free information? If some guy on Youtube can *really* teach you how to build a profitable business, would he do it for free? In all likelihood, their free information is just misinformation that'll set you back from success.

Mistake number three: unrealistic expectations.

If you've spent five minutes Googling about internet marketing, you've probably been hit with promises about getting rich quick. There's a lot of false promises out there about "six figures in six days" or "easy seven-figure product launches" without proof to back any of it up.

It's easy to have unrealistic expectations about online business success. For example, most of the million-dollar success stories you hear about rely on million-dollar advertising budgets. If breaking even is considered success, I'd hate to see failure!

Compare visions of grandeur with the digital agency opportunity. It's much more practical. If this book marks your first entry into a digital business, you're starting where I wish I would've started back in 2000. If your agency can make a few clients happy through ROI on your services, they'll want to keep you. Then they'll refer you to their buddies. And once you're up to about a dozen clients who each pay between $1,000 and $3,000 per month, all sales pressure is gone. Your business becomes an annuity, paying out month after month with very little upkeep. No "Get Rich Quick" scheme offers this kind of luxury.

In my program Agency FastTrack, we've helped many everyday people launch high ROI agencies by teaching the right skills at the right time. I'll be transparent; nobody is getting rich quick, but many of them are on track for $10,000 to $20,000 monthly revenue in twelve months or less. And unlike expensive product launches, the digital agency profit margin is much higher. In your agency, you'll have very, very few expenses to budget for: a laptop and a Wifi connection, which you probably have already!

Another unrealistic expectation to do away with is what I call **Damascus Decision-Making**. It goes like this:

Whether you're new to digital marketing or not, you'll have to learn many new technologies over the course of your career so you can advise your clients on which program, which software, and which platform is best for their business.

For example, when you're building a website, you'll have to decide whether to build a WordPress site, Squarespace, Wix, or any of twenty other Content Management System (CMS) platforms. If you spend a couple of hours evaluating each, two or three days are gone, and chances are, you won't make a good decision. Then you'll need a landing page builder and an email campaign tool. Can't forget about those!

The decision-making never stops. If you rely on your own judgment to pick a Goldilocks technology—one that's "just right"—you'll end up spending eighty percent of your time evaluating different technologies, not actually building a business.

As the saying goes, "all roads lead to Damascus." So just pick one, and take it! Don't expect to test every path to find out for yourself which is shortest, or none of them will be. Don't let decision-making paralyze you from making progress. Whether it's a website, landing page, or email, find something that does the job, and run like mad to Damascus.

Mistake number four: underestimated skills.

By now, you know businesses will hire you for one thing—return on investment. Creating ROI is more than knowing a technology well, like Facebook Ads or Google Ads. Most aspiring agency owners start by learning a technology, but the problem is, technologies change way too fast. When Google's SEO algorithm changed, Twitter ended lead ads, and Myspace marketing went the way of the dinosaur, marketers on those platforms lost everything, starting with their clients.

If you paid attention to social media headlines in early 2018, you saw another disaster play out. In January, Facebook announced major changes to brand content promotions, which left countless social media post specialists jobless. Then when the Cambridge Analytica privacy fiasco hit headlines, Facebook lost $100 billion in ten days and put a temporary hold on new messenger bots.[1,2] If your agency specialized in Messenger Bot services, Facebook's privacy issue left you in dire straits.

Clearly, knowing a platform isn't enough to ensure digital agency success. And having the skills to use a platform *effectively* isn't enough either. But there is one ageless, timeless skill that drives every high ROI advertising campaign.

Strategy.

To convert a random website browser into a loyal customer, you've got to be a *strategist*. You've got to blend the right offer, the right audience, the right landing page, the right copy, the right ads, and the right call-to-action, all of which look different for each client. It's easy to learn technical skills, but mastering strategy can be challenging. (Fortunately, this book makes it much, much easier! The next nine chapters are NOTHING but strategy.)

Mistake number five: false trends.

A shovel isn't gold, and a toy isn't an opportunity. Many agency owners keep tabs on the headlines like a broker watches his stocks, waiting patiently for something new and exciting to come along. For months, Messenger Bots seemed to be the new trend. Agencies popped up all over North America overnight to capitalize. Then when the new thing was no longer the new thing, those agencies were toast.

As you learn the strategies of high ROI marketing, keep both eyes on the essentials—Audiences (Chapter 4), Campaigns (Chapter 5), and Funnels (Chapter 6). Toys come and go, but winning strategies are forever. Real trends worth pursuing are based on mass movements, such as sustained marketing spending increases. If something can come and go in a few months (like bots), they're not a real trend.

Mistake number six: marketing misunderstandings.

It drives me crazy how very, very few professional marketers actually know anything about marketing. Marketing is a *process*, not an event. Done right, marketing is a series of romantic dates where each partner builds trust on their way to a lifetime of intimacy, romance, and passion. Done wrong, marketing is a marriage proposal on the first date...before the appetizers.

The telling question every bad marketer asks is, "How can I get clients?" Whatever their answer is, it's usually pushy, salesy, and expensive. **First Date Proposal Marketing** is a PPC ad driving traffic to a website in hopes that somebody buys on the spot. But think about it—nobody actually wants to marry the type of person who's willing to accept a stranger's marriage proposal on the first date!

In contrast, **Dating To Marry Marketing** asks a different question, "How can I get clients *to stay with me*?" You approach every interaction with customers like it's a relationship. Your job is to present a low-risk offer inside of a funnel (first date) so a person buys a product or service once, then again and again and again (marriage). As a digital agency owner, it's your job to teach your clients what marketing is (and is not) so they'll become indispensable to their target market, which makes you indispensable to them.

Mistake number seven: naiveté.

If you don't know what you're getting yourself into, your business won't make it. My mentor Russell Brunson once told me, "There is a ninety-five percent chance anything you do the first time will fail." I completely agree.

On the first day of Agency FastTrack, I repeat Russell's wisdom to my students. To this day, I'm surprised when more than one person replies, "Don't worry, Niel. I don't intend to fail." I always crack a smile. **Naiveté is the enemy of progress.** Building a successful agency is hard work. Nobody does everything perfect the first time, whether it's designing a landing page or writing an ad headline. That includes me.

If you're willing to fail, if you're willing to try again, if you're willing to keep learning until it sticks, then you have what it takes to succeed. This attitude is what pioneer psychologist Carol Dweck calls "the growth mindset."[3]

As a digital agency entrepreneur, you're going to get frustrated. So laugh at yourself. You're going to have your face glued to a screen all day. So take frequent breaks. You're going to make mistakes with your clients. So hold yourself accountable and fix them.

Mistake number eight: the wrong measure of success.

"But our Facebook posts get lots of engagement… But we built you a great website… But you're getting lots of organic views…"

Small business owners hear these excuses when they chew out their marketing team for poor results. As a marketer, if you measure success based on ANYTHING other than ROI, your services are irrelevant. If you don't produce return on a client's investment, you deserve to be fired. Rather black and white, isn't it? You bet. Ruthless accountability isn't for the faint of heart.

CHAPTER 2 - THE 12 MISTAKES EVERY NEWBIE MAKES (THAT YOU DON'T HAVE TO)

Put yourself in SMB owners' shoes. Do they want to pay for "social engagement," "a great website," or "views?" Snake oil salesmen might be able to rationalize why a business *should* pay for these, and many do. But at the end of the month when a business owner asks, "Is this person's services making me money?" the answer is either yes or no.

Mistake number nine: corporations over SMBs.

In the United States, there are over 120,000 marketing agencies, all clambering to get the latest large corporate account, of which there are very few. **See the big red problem?** A bloody, competitive ocean where many, many sharks fight over fewer and fewer prey. No one-man or one-woman agency has a chance in that market. So don't swim in those waters. Instead, target local small businesses. Not big businesses, corporations, or Fortune 500s. They're a blue ocean ignored by the big agencies with big expenses (offices, teams, etc.)

A corporate client may pay their digital agency $100,000 per year, but the owner is lucky to get a ten percent profit margin. To compare, you'll aim for a dozen SMB clients who each pay you between $1,000 and $3,000 per month at a ninety percent-plus profit margin. Think small, win big.

Mistake number ten: freelancing.

You can be a successful freelancer, or you can run a successful digital agency, but you can't do both. My simple rule is this: whatever you can hire someone on Fiverr to do, your agency shouldn't. Freelancers, by definition, accept once-off, commissioned, personalized freelance work. When the website is done, the content is published, the podcast is edited...you're toast. You're like an ancient hunter-gatherer with no refrigerator, eating whatever you can find, kill, or uproot that day. The next morning, the battle starts all over again.

Come to the twenty-first century. Offer a monthly retainer service that gives your clients consistent value, and you a sustainable business.

Mistake number eleven: client briefs.

I've got news for you. Your clients don't have the first clue what their marketing and advertising needs are. So why would you ask them? Yet most agency owners do *exactly* that. Before getting started with a client, the agency requests a Client Brief, a document that includes the business' current marketing strategy, campaign goals, target market data, competitor info, and recyclable marketing materials.

Only one problem. We're talking about hairdressers. Landscapers. Plumbers. Personal trainers. Dentists. They don't know anything about Client Briefs. None of their job descriptions include a peep about digital marketing strategy. Not one.

Never assume a client knows what they need or has what they need. In most cases, any and all past campaigns they've run *sucked*! From you, your clients need strong, strategic leadership. They need to know what is the right tactic to advertise their business online and what isn't. They need a growth partner with high ROI strategies, not a services catalog to pick and choose from.

Mistake number twelve: platform confusion.

Repeat after me: "Facebook is not Google; Google is not Facebook."

Great. Now let me explain why this distinction matters to anyone who wants to create high ROI marketing campaigns. While billions of people use their Facebook accounts and search Google on the same day—or in some cases, within the same thirty seconds—the *context* of each platform means strategic marketers should treat them very, very differently.

My coaching business, Agency FastTrack, makes this distinction bright as the sun. On Google, I want my company in front of people *already* searching for how they can either start a digital agency or what they should look out for when choosing a great business opportunity. Because if you're searching for a product or service online, chances are you're in shopping cart mode. You're "scanning the aisles" for the right program, and I want you to choose Agency FastTrack. Therefore every Google ad I run drives traffic to a page where I share a lot of valuable content on how to start and run a highly profitable digital agency, and why it's probably one of the best business opportunities right now!

If I repurpose this strategy for my Facebook ads, I probably won't sell one course. On Facebook, users scroll their news feeds for the latest cat videos to share and political arguments to join. They're not in shopping cart mode. In many cases, the audiences I'm targeting have never even considered starting their own digital agency. So before I pitch my product, I have to build context by explaining why here is a HUGE untapped market for digital lead generation agencies globally. (More on building context and educating customers in Chapter 4.)

To put it simply, Google is about relevance, and Facebook is about interruption. On Google, a search brings up relevant product results. On Facebook, marketers interrupt users to provoke curiosity. In many cases, Facebook advertisers have to first educate users and build relevance in their minds. Confusing who uses which platforms for what only confuses how to use each platform to create ROI.

Every one of these **Top Twelve Digital Agency Beginner Mistakes** probably seems, well, *obvious*. But when you're in the thick of growing your agency, acquiring the skills, and mastering the strategy, you'll be able to spot the traps your competitors won't. So while everyone else sells the farm and gives up, you'll own a successful, sustainable operation to mine the digital agency opportunity for everything it's worth—and build a successful, sustainable business in the process nearly mistake-free.

So now that you know what NOT to do, you're ready to start digging. And start building.

CHAPTER 3

YOUR HIGH ROI BUSINESS MODEL

Building a business is hard work. Just ask your clients. They start their businesses for more reasons than straight up wealth creation. SMBs come with an emotional attachment that corporations do not. To even the most ambitious owners, small businesses are a labor of love and self-expression. They want to have an impact on the world while also putting their kids through college. Like one hundred percent commission salespeople, owners' livelihoods depend on their performance alone. Excuses do them no good.

Entrepreneurship is a difficult journey where every battle is winner-takes-all. And on that journey, YOU, the digital agency, are the small business owner's godsend. You're not just in the business of providing a service, selling marketing, or running ads. You're *really* in the business of helping Moms and Pops grow their little companies into something extraordinary. To SMBs, you are what marketing godfather Seth Godin calls, the "**linchpin**."[1]

Usually a linchpin refers to somebody of importance, but I can't think of a better way to define your role as a digital agency than the *original* definition...

During the Middle Ages, the wheel drove all commerce. Literally! As the greatest technology of its time, the wheel served society through its thousands of uses in agriculture, cookware, fashion, and transportation, to name a few.

Have you ever seen a wheel up close? A wheel rotates on a central shaft called an axle. But without a tiny fastener, the wheel flies off its axle, the vehicle goes mad, and the driver loses all control. In Middle English, that fastener—the little device which keeps the whole world safe—is called a "*lynspin*."[2]

Linchpin.

That's what your digital agency is to your clients. You're the protector of their deepest desires. Without the steady flow of new leads and customers your advertising drives into their business, the profit wheels fly off the wagon, and the owner's dreams crash and burn.

Yes, even a one-man or one-woman show—you and your agency—means *that much* to a small business. You keep SMBs rolling forward into the future by answering the most difficult question an owner can ask:

"How do I find more customers?"

Your high ROI services answer that question for them so they can focus on growing their business, serving their people, and making a contribution to the world. That's why the digital agency opportunity is as much of a gold mine for small businesses as it is for aspiring entrepreneurs like you. The fact is, most businesses never reach their full potential because they never have enough customers; they remain their industry's best-kept secret, then the wheels come off and that's it. Sad.

This bleak future stares into small business owner Little Joe's eyes every morning when he opens up shop for the day. *Will this be the day the customers stop coming? Will this be the day everything falls apart?*

Then along comes your digital agency. You're Little Joe's strategic partner, change agent, and growth enabler. From here on out, most of the business' successes will be because of *you*. Through your high ROI advertising services, you'll create a near endless flow of new business that propels Little Joe toward success he once thought impossible. In return, he'll enjoy paying you as much as you enjoy getting paid—maybe even more so.

Eventually, with your help, Little Joe the small business owner becomes industry-dominating Big Joe whose business needs even *more* services, from branding and a website to custom applications and PR campaigns. And so, your own business grows with Big Joe's.

CHAPTER 3 - YOUR HIGH ROI BUSINESS MODEL

This is the golden road ahead of you, but your prosperous adventure starts with a high return on your services—lead generation and customer acquisition, specifically. Not hours worked. Not deliverables created. High ROI. If Little Joe *knows* he'll make three hundred bucks when he spends two hundred with you—three thousand when he spends one thousand and so on—you've got him for life.

With so much profit at stake for you and small business clients like Little Joe, you can't afford to bumble into the industry, boost a few posts on Facebook, and hope Little Joe's phone rings off the hook. Your job is to make more money for him than you do for yourself. Not the most motivating message, I know, but that's where the bar of digital agency success firmly sits, and there's no budging it.

The only way to meet Little Joe's high ROI standard is to devise an effective strategy, a proven one that's virtually guaranteed to win before you deploy your first ad. Like the great Chinese military strategist Sun Tzu wrote, "Victorious warriors win first and then go to war."

That's why I wrote this book. From identifying the right **Audience** of prospects (Chapter 4) to deploying the right advertising **Message** (Chapter 5) to driving traffic through a sales-generating **Funnel** (Chapter 6), your strategic approach will turn your clients' profit wheels faster and faster.

While the end results of your strategy are more leads, more sales, and more customers, your very **first conversation** with a client should have nothing to do with the loads of cash you'll bring into the business.

Strategy starts with **clarity**, and clarity comes through **questions**. In my Agency FastTrack program, I have students ask every new practice client three questions. (These questions alone have an incredible impact on your potential clients. Your value goes up in their eyes because they've most likely thought about these questions, just never pursued answers. More importantly, these questions matter because, left unanswered, they prevent your agency from playing the linchpin role.)

Of course, you're going to charge clients an initial set up fee for answering these questions and building strategies around their answers. But because you're in business to grow their business, they'll be happy to pay.

Question number one: **"Who is your ideal customer and why?"**

Small business owners battle to answer this question because more seems better. "Shouldn't everyone buy my product or need my service?" your clients will ask you.

No. No, they shouldn't. And that's a *good* thing—according to the Pareto Principle, roughly twenty percent of a customer base drives eighty percent of a business' sales. Management consultant and efficiency expert Richard Koch makes crystal clear how serving "everyone" weakens SMBs' ability to grow:

> [T]he 80/20 Principle asserts that 20 percent of products, or customers...are really responsible for about 80 percent of profits. If this is true...the state of affairs implied is very far from being efficient or optimal. The implication is that 80 percent of products, or customers...are only contributing 20 percent of profits; that there is great waste; that the most powerful resources of the company are being held back by a majority of much less effective resources; that profits could be multiplied if more of the best sort of products could be sold...or customers attracted (or convinced to buy more from the firm).[3]

Understanding who is and who is not a good customer is critical to advertising success. Unfortunately, most SMB owners advertise to "everyone" and end up acquiring customers who *don't* fit into that twenty percent ideal customer category. They end up wasting precious time, energy, and resources servicing customers who don't really profit them that much.

For example, in my business Elite Inc., I sell a $600 program and a $6,500 program. Based on that price difference, you might assume the higher priced program costs more to advertise.

You'd be wrong. About twenty percent of my customers buy my $6,500 program, but their purchases accounts for *at least* eighty percent of company revenue. If your digital agency had Elite Inc. as a client, you'd want to know as much about that program's audience as possible.

The higher the advertising ROI, the easier your job is, the better you justify investing in your services.

You'll notice the Pareto Principle manifest in your own client base. A one-person business that makes $100,000 per year might be able to pay you $500 a month for your services. Or maybe not. But a small to medium sized business hauling in $300,000 up to $1 million per year is big enough to afford a digital agency like yours at $2,000 to $3,000 per month. Which type of business do you want to spend your time pursuing?

In Chapter 4, I'll teach you exactly how to strategize which **Audience** of buyers your clients should pursue. For now, keep question number one in your front pocket so you'll be ready at a moment's notice to set your clients on the road to ROI from your very first conversation.

Question number two: **"What makes your business truly unique?"**

In 2010, two guys met at a party and bonded over a shared frustration—razor blade shopping. Razors are so damn expensive and inconvenient, they agreed. That first conversation over cocktails sparked another and another. *What if razor blades were affordable? What if shopping for them was convenient?*

Over the next year, the two guys answered both questions through plans for a truly unique product in the centuries-old, billion-dollar industry of men's grooming products. Dollar Shave Club was born.[4] Within five years, the co-founders sold the business for a *billion* dollars.[5]

Now, the lesson here for small business owners isn't to go mad and sell razor blades. What made Dollar Shave Club so successful so fast was hyper-specific messaging, which promoted the company's monthly razor blade subscription product over and over and over. So while every other razor blade collected dust on retail shelves, Dollar Shave Club blades appeared on customers' porches at a reasonable price the same day every month. Win-win.

Help your clients determine what makes them the Dollar Shave Club of their industry, and put that unique feature at the center of their **Messaging**. A client's business may not sell for hundreds of millions, but with all those new customers banging their doors down, they'll *feel* like a billion bucks!

Question number three: **"What does success look like?"**

Before you get to work on a client's campaign, help them define *exactly* what success looks like. Is your **Funnel** successful when the business gets ten prospect calls a day? When you've tripled their return on advertising expenses? When they've closed the maximum number of sales they can handle in a single month?

You might even ask your clients, "How will we both know the campaign was a success?" If your client sets up a target *before* you create the very first ad, you are that much more likely to hit it. Your digital agency may not be all about you, but when you create a winning, high ROI strategy for your clients, you'll feel like it is...I guarantee it.

CHAPTER 4

YOUR FIRST HIGH ROI STRATEGY: AUDIENCES

You're sitting across the table from a small business owner.

"Who are your ideal customers?" you ask her.

"Well..." She thinks for a moment. "Everyone, I guess."

"Okay, let's narrow that down a bit," you say. "What type of customer produces the most profit for you but takes the least amount of time and effort to find?"

She names a few long-time customers from memory. "On average, I'd say they buy about two hundred dollars' worth of product every time they come into my store. Profit is roughly fifty percent."

"Great, so fifty dollars per transaction," you say. "How does that compare to your average customer? Or even," you smile, "your *least* ideal customer?"

"Well..." She frowns. "My regulars buy probably ten to fifteen dollars' worth, and my least ideal customers buy a stick of gum every time they come in."

"So there's a difference between customers whose transactions are worth fifty *dollars* and those worth *fifty* cents."

"Oh, yes! They're completely different types of people," your prospect says.

And the light bulb goes off.

"So what you're implying is," she nods, "we should target only the type of customers who make me the most money, and we should go and find more of them?"

"Yes!" You see a deal approach on a silver platter.

Then she asks *you* a few questions.

"Okay then," her arms cross, "so how do I find more of these people? And how do I market to them so they buy from me and not my competitor across the street?"

"..."

You sit there, staring.

How DO I find more of her ideal customers? And how do I convince them to buy from HER?

You say nothing. Because you don't know. *Yet.*

****

Let's pause that scene. As you build your digital agency, you're going to have conversations just like this one over and over and over.

And your prospect will expect you to have the answers she needs.

If there's anything I *don't* want for you, it's that you answer a question with a question.

"I don't know how to find out who your ideal customers are. Do you?" That question definitely won't fly!

But when you sit across from SMB owners and lay out a process to determine *exactly* who their ideal customers are *and* how ready they are to buy, these owners will be happy to write you a check on the spot.

The **first step** in your process to create a coherent Audience Strategy that helps ensure your campaigns reach and convert those high value twenty percent customers, is the **Avatar**. (To get an Avatar sheet like the one from the example below, go to EliteInc.com/AgencyBookResources.)

CHAPTER 4 - YOUR FIRST HIGH ROI STRATEGY: AUDIENCES

HIGH ROI GENERATING
WORKING MOM CUSTOMER AVATAR SHEET

GET TO KNOW YOUR IDEAL CUSTOMER INSIDE AND OUT.
USE YOUR AVATARS TO LAUNCH HIGH ROI DIGITAL MARKETING CAMPAIGNS.
READY? LETS MEET YOUR CUSTOMER!

DEMOGRAPHICS

- Works long hours, looking for flexibility
- 35 - Early 40's in a Corporate / Managerial Position
- Female
- Married, with Kids not yet in High School

$100k Annual Income

Quote that defines them

I am a mom working myself to death and achieving nothing so it's time to change and digital is the future. I would love to build a successful digital company to hand down to my children to secure their futures.

GOALS AND VALUES

Values
Family-oriented, hard-working, committed

Goals
Wants to be able to spend more time with their kids

CHALLENGES AND PAIN POINTS:

- **Challenge** — Fear based - I need money to make money
- **Challenge** — Cost of starting a business
- **Challenge** — Fear of failure
- **Pain point** — I need to be able to financially support my family, but also enjoy leisure time with them

OBJECTIONS

- **Objection** — I feel like I've missed the boat missed the opportunity in digital and can't catch up
- **Objection** — I need job security
- **Objection** — How long will it take before I start making money?
- **Objection** — Will I be able to do this?

HELLO I'M YOUR IDEAL CUSTOMER. NICE TO MEET YOU.

BUILDING YOUR AVATAR CORRECTLY IS ONE OF THE MOST IMPORTANT TOOLS FOR
BUILDING THE AGENCY-CLIENT RELATIONSHIP.

 Elite Inc.

If your clients' customers were characters in a movie, an Avatar is each character's bio. (Didn't think owning an agency meant becoming a biographer, did you?)

Once you know *how* to create an Avatar, you and your clients' jaws will drop as you realize how much easier your Avatars make it to launch high ROI campaigns.

Each Avatar includes all the data you'd need to know about a business' ideal customer if you wanted to pick them out of a crowd. For example, is the customer male or female? How old are they? Do they live in a specific geographic area? How educated are they? What are their top life priorities?

In Agency FastTrack, I teach students to ask clients about four specific categories that, together, make a complete customer Avatar picture. (To get my free Facebook Targeting Guide to build an Avatar-based audience, go to EliteInc.com/AgencyBookResources.)

Demographics is a "just the facts" category, which includes customer age, gender, location, marital status, children, occupation, industry, income, and education. For example, one of my ideal Agency FastTrack customers is Olivia, a forty year-old, high income-earning mom with a demanding career and two school-age children.

The **Psychographics** category relates to attitudes, behaviors, and ways of thinking, including customer goals, wants, needs, passions, revulsions, fears, drivers, and current challenges. Olivia has been working long hours and missing out on her kids lives. She needs the flexibility to be able to go to their sport games or help them with their homework while still contributing financially to the family.

The **Influencer** category is based on what influences a customer's thinking and behavior, like certain books, magazines, websites, blogs, groups, and experts. Olivia attends business and leadership courses, likes to expand her knowledge through online learning, and subscribes to popular business blogs and newsletters she finds on Google.

The last category, for lack of a better term, is **objections to the sale** and includes everything that might stop your Avatar from actually taking the next step with you. Olivia might be scared that she's missed the boat in terms of understanding and mastering digital marketing, and she doesn't have the luxury of not contributing to the family finances.

Feel like you know Olivia personally, don't you? Like you could have a cup of coffee with her and talk about her family, her aspirations, and her goals.

That's how you know you've built your Avatar correctly. With your own clients, the Avatar building workshop is one of your most important tools for building the agency-client relationship. During this meeting, keep it simple. Walk the business owner through all four customer Avatar categories. Help them complete the categories as best they can relying on past experiences with customers as well as their current customer database.

As questions get answered and the categories fill up, your client will experience clarity unlike any they've ever had as a business owner. By the end of the Avatar workshop, you and your client have a complete picture of their ideal customer, what makes them tick, and why they're likely to buy your client's product.

But just *how* likely are they to purchase once, then again, and remain a customer for life? To answer that question, you'll need to take the **second step** in the Audience Strategy Process, R.E.A.D.Y.

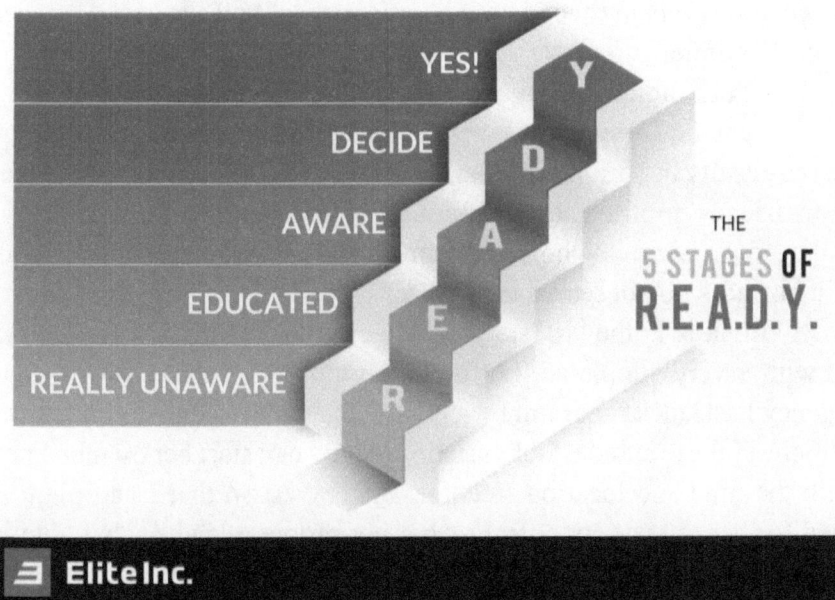

Whether your clients believe it or not, not *every* ideal customer of theirs is "ready" to buy right now. Some are newer to the industry. Others haven't assessed their needs to figure out what product they really want. And some go mad with a Do It Yourself solution before joining reality and realizing they're better off buying a solution that already exists.

As your clients' growth partner, you have expertise your clients rely on to pursue their ideal customers in a way that's most likely to convert them into buyers. What I call the **Five Stages of R.E.A.D.Y.** is your secret weapon to do just that. (For a detailed version of the Five Stages, go to EliteInc.com/AgencyBookResources.)

In any market, customers' varying readiness to buy a product places them in one of five stages. Depending on the stage—and consequently their interest in buying your client's product—you'll use a different platform to market to them. Let's dig into the differences.

Stage One: Really Unaware

"R" stage customers are **really unaware** of...well, everything! At this point in the buying cycle, these customers haven't even realized they have a problem, and therefore aren't ready for a solution. They're what we refer to as "cold," which means they are probably not going to be receptive to being faced with an offer straight off the bat! They need some "warming" up first.

Will your digital agency use Facebook or Google to reach them?

Remember, **Google is relevance**, **Facebook is interruption**. Google search results list information and product links, Facebook news feeds show friends' profile changes, popular videos, and fan page updates to name a few. The right choice is clear. Customers who aren't even *aware* of a business do not search Google for it!

If Olivia is in the "R" stage of her customer journey, I'll warm her up with a very simple ad, but definitely not an ad that showcases the Agency FastTrack program. I want Olivia to make a connection between her stressful life and the fact that she actually can start her own business, with the time and location freedom she craves, so that I can plant the seed for her to start connecting what her problem is and what solution she should be considering.

So my Facebook Ad will show a stock image of an early forty-something lady staring out her office window with multiple stacks of papers on her desk with one line of text, something like: "Are you tired of missing out on time with your kids because you're working all the time?" and a link to a blog post about how you can take back your life and unlock your financial future. One glance at this ad, and a light bulb goes off for Olivia. She now starts understanding that her missing out on her kids' lives because she's permanently stuck in the office is actually her problem, and that there is a solution that she needs to find.

If I did want to cover Google as well, I would run a Google Ads search campaign for searches like "work/life balance" or "flexi jobs." To get Olivia interested in my product, my ad leads her to an article about the unlocked opportunity of starting her own business, where she can get in touch with me should she need more help.

Stage Two: Educated

"E" stage customers have **educated** themselves about their problem, need, or goal. They know they have one, so they're asking friends, scrolling their newsfeeds, and searching Google for answers.

Thanks to my Facebook ad, Olivia knows her real problem is the fact that she needs a job with location and time freedom that still helps her to contribute financially to the family, so she opens Google. "Location and time freedom jobs," she types, followed by "laptop lifestyle," and "how to start your own business," to compare her options.

While my competitors' product ads appear in the search results for expensive keywords not directly related to Olivia's search, I want her to know that she can run a virtual business that gives her complete time, location, and financial freedom. That's why my ad appears in the top of the results for keywords focused around *starting your own business* and why it drives traffic to a blog article on the untapped opportunity of starting and running your own business.

I also start planting the seed about the fact that she doesn't need to go on this path alone— that I have a shortcut for her. And a foolproof one at that. I want to reassure her that I'll be with her every step of the way, and I will not let her fail.

Stage Three: Aware

"A" stage customers are **aware** of the result they want. They see very, very clearly a future where their problem is solved, their need is met, their goal is achieved. But they're clueless about your client's product, so it's your job to craft a clever message about it and slide it across their radar—AKA their screen.

At this point in my advertising campaign, I've made Olivia aware of the fact that she needs a time and location free job so that she can spend more time with her kids, while still contributing financially to the family. It's now time that Olivia learns that there is a huge untapped market for digital agencies globally, and how she can start and run her very own.

On Facebook, I run a short, ten-second video ad which explains how with the rights skills and mentoring, Olivia will be able to actually realize her dream of being time and location independent. Note how the message isn't an ad for Agency FastTrack specifically, it's an ad for the *exact* solution Olivia needs. Of course, she can't help but see my company branding in the video, so now she knows Agency FastTrack exists. Success!

To cover Olivia's stage-specific Google searches, I run Google Ads for "digital marketing," "lead generation," and "digital agencies." These ads then send her to an article where she learns about how she could soon be living the laptop lifestyle by starting her very own digital agency.

I also reiterate that the power to take back her life and be in control of her own destiny is within her grasp! And that she just needs to reach out and grab it. That it is absolutely possible to live and work location free. To find a satisfying career that works around her, instead of her around it. I nudge Olivia that I want to give her the work-life balance she's been craving, but never actually thought she could achieve. And all she has to do is attend a free webinar.

Stage Four: Decide

"D" stage customers are aware that they have a problem, but they may not be convinced that your product or service is the solution to their problem. At this stage of the buying cycle, prospects are closer to a decision and are in **deliberation mode.** Now your advertising objective

CHAPTER 4 - YOUR FIRST HIGH ROI STRATEGY: AUDIENCES

is to show your audience how *your client's* product, *not* the competition, meets all their criteria.

With my last Facebook ad, I've turned Olivia's world upside-down. I've shown her the fastest, most proven, least expensive way to get her to that elusive time and location freedom. Olivia is now ready for Agency FastTrack. So in my very first ad, I feature a photo of Olivia lying by the beach with her laptop by her side, watching her kids play in the sand, with a provocative Avatar-specific headline, something like, "Work location free and earn up to $10K getting leads online." One click later, and Olivia is reading an article that explains the top ten reasons my program is the best on the market. On Google, I'm finally ready to go after product-specific keywords like "start my digital agency" and even competitors' brands and product names. Only because *Olivia* is ready.

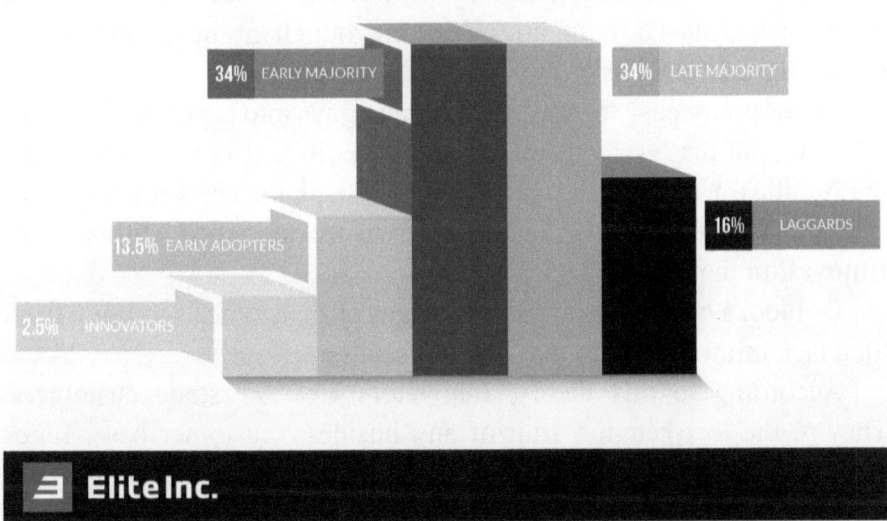

Stage Five: Yes!

"**Y**" stage customers are ready to say, "**YES!**" to the product or service that's earned their credit card—your client's product or service. If a customer makes a purchase, any purchase, they do so with their gut.

So speak to their gut! It's only human to buy on emotion, then justify with logic, so the very last thing a wise marketer does is send traffic to a page with endless bullet points and product specs so that all purchase dissonance is removed.

In "Y" stage, Olivia is falling off the fence. I want her falling off that fence into the Agency FastTrack program! On Facebook, I run another video ad, this one featuring a satisfied customer named Megan—who happens to be an early forties businesswoman who has taken her destiny back into her own hands by leaving the corporate rat race, and actually living the dream of time, location, and financial freedom. In thirty seconds or less, Megan pulls Olivia's emotions off the fence. She has investigated other business opportunities, but going through the Agency FastTrack program has given her the results she's been looking for. She's finally able to cheer her kids on next to the field, set her own hours, and still contribute well to the household finances.

Before the video ends, Olivia tears through her wallet to find her credit card. Boom! (Of course, any product or service testimonial you feature in ads must be authentic. *Never* let your clients buy, bribe, or beg to get fake testimonials!)

Looks pretty easy to convert "Y" stage guys into customers, doesn't it? It is! And that's exactly what makes credit-card-in-hand customers the Achilles' Heel of a digital agency. I'll explain. The Five Stages of R.E.A.D.Y. naturally overlaps a different model called **Diffusion of Innovation** theory (DoI).[1]

DoI looks *backwards* at the five stages of a customer's journey from total lack of awareness to that first transaction.

According to this theory, Innovators are "Y" stage customers. They're the low-hanging fruit of any business' customer base. Innovators are the first to buy anything and require the least effort on your agency's part to reach. It's easy to publish a Facebook ad that drives "Y" stage customers to a sales page. So easy, in fact, that most agencies create campaigns that target *only* these Innovators, ignoring everyone else who isn't ready to buy right this second. Sure, your client will be happy with an immediate influx of business, but two or three months later, the well's dried up and so has their advertising budget.

CHAPTER 4 - YOUR FIRST HIGH ROI STRATEGY: AUDIENCES

Nearly a decade ago, marketing legend Chet Holmes explained why "Yes" stage-only campaigns fail so quickly in his book *The Ultimate Sales Machine*. It's math:

> About 3 percent of potential buyers at any given time are buying now. Right now.[2]

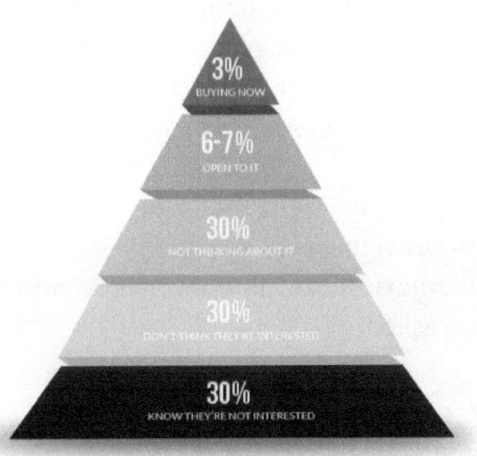

That's it. No business can sustain itself on such a tiny portion of its customer base. Yet that's *exactly* where most agencies start and stay. When that three percent is all tapped out, your competitors lose their clients...*to you*.

You have a comprehensive Audience Strategy. *You* can identify SMBs' most valuable customers and distill all of their characteristics into a single customer bio, the Avatar. And *you* know how to reach the remaining ninety-seven percent of a business' customer base—the Early Adopters (Deciding Customers), Early Majority (Solution-Aware Customers), Late Majority (Problem-Educated Customers), and Laggards (Really Unaware Customers).

Your competitors never had a chance. They don't know the Diffusion of Innovation and haven't read this book, so they probably accept what's called the "Marketing Rule of Seven" at face value. This marketing industry conventional wisdom goes like this:

> A prospect needs to see or hear an advertiser's message at least 7 times before they'll buy.[3]

Simple enough, right? Write a product sales page ad, run it to an audience seven times, and we're home before dinner. That's what most agency owners think. But message repetition simply isn't enough. With the Five Stages of R.E.A.D.Y. in the back of your mind, you're thinking, *Hold on! Repetition is great, but customers at different stages respond to a different message.*

And you're right. So what exactly *are* those different messages? How do you craft the right stage-specific message so customers in that stage move to the next stage...and the next...and the next...and then *buy*? I'm glad you asked.

CHAPTER 5

YOUR SECOND HIGH ROI STRATEGY: MESSAGING

Most digital agency owners I meet believe product quality trumps product messaging. That's why marketers spend all their time mastering the tech of advertising campaigns—landing page coding, email autoresponders, ad management software...the list goes on. They leave a few minutes here and there for brainstorming their ads' content, if that. A lot of agency owners actually expect their *clients* to come up with the messaging! That's like a physician diagnosing a patient, then asking said patient to perform their own surgery.

Remember the eighty-twenty principle? It also applies to the Messaging Strategy you implement for your clients. If you're going to make the most of the digital agency opportunity, do the exact opposite of the guys who don't know anything about Tracking Pixels—spend eighty percent of your time brainstorming ad headlines, landing page content, and product copy, then spend twenty percent of your time learning how to use advertising technologies. Mastering those technologies won't do you much good without eye-catching content. Nobody buys a product because the sales page margins are the exact perfect width. For example, improving just one sentence—the headline—can result in conversion increases anywhere from twelve percent to higher than one hundred percent.[1,2]

I believe messaging is not an afterthought, it's *the* thought. British copywriter David Ogilvy, billed as the "father of advertising," set the standard for us all:

> On the average, five times as many people read the headline as read the body copy. When you have written your headline, you have spent eighty cents out of your dollar...As a matter of fact I try to write twenty alternative headlines for every advertisement.[3]

Although Ogilvy reached his prime decades ago, his ideas live on into the Digital Age. He believed that successful advertising for any product is based on information about its customer. Sound familiar?

Messaging is the most timeless aspect of any agency's services. Tech changes, but human beings don't. We can't resist a good headline. It's almost like our species evolved to respond to advertising that tells a story! Because we *did*. Other than stone tools, cave paintings are the oldest remnants of our hunter-gatherer ancestors. Tens of thousands of years ago, people painted caves across modern-day Africa, Europe, Australia, the Americas, and Asia to tell their stories—stories of families loved, beasts hunted, and gods worshipped.

Even in our fast-paced, smartphone-enabled world, whenever we hear the words, "Let me tell you a story," we perk up. We tune in. We pay attention. So wrap your clients' Messaging Strategy around human nature. People respond to headlines, stories, narrative, not plain old facts about a business or product. That's why so many agencies cannot turn a client's hundred bucks into three hundred. They might have heard a thing or two about Avatars, but their persuasion expertise ends there.

You, on the other hand, are a small business' greatest asset. You know exactly *who* their highest ROI customers are and, by the end of this chapter, you know exactly *how* to move them from unaware shopper to loyal buyer. To create ad campaigns that do just that, you need **a twofold Messaging Strategy**.

CHAPTER 5 - YOUR SECOND HIGH ROI STRATEGY: MESSAGING

First, you need to know what constitutes a great message, full stop. **Second**, you need to know what constitutes a great message for *each* of the Five Stages.

First, a great message: What makes an ad work is the simplest, yet most complex lesson in all of marketing. Ready? In our digital world, you have more to work with than letters and pictures on a page. David Ogilvy had newspapers, magazines, and posters; you have Facebook image ads, Facebook video ads, Google Ads headlines and links, and landing pages to create all the content your heart desires. Regardless of platform or industry, the anatomy of a high ROI ad is quite simple.

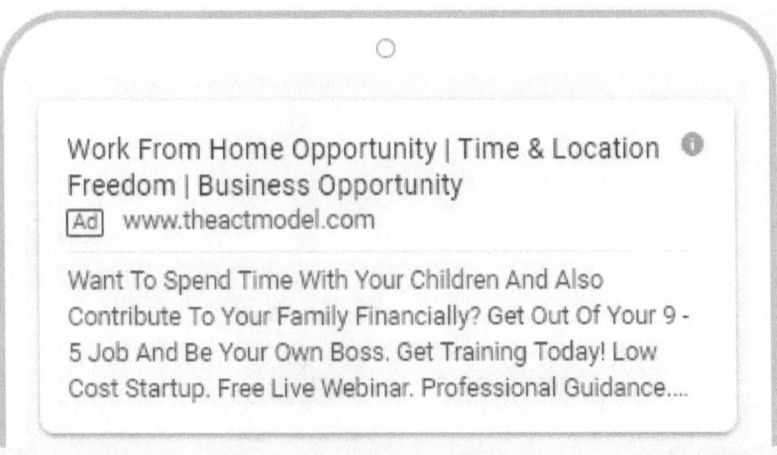

On the two most common websites you'll run ads on for your clients, you've got a headline, the starting point of every call-to-action. On Facebook, you have space for an image or video, a button, and copy that expands on your headline.

On both platforms, your only job is to get a click. That's it. The click. Nobody sells a product from a single ad, not even David Ogilvy. There is *always* a next step. For digital campaigns, that next step is a **landing page**.

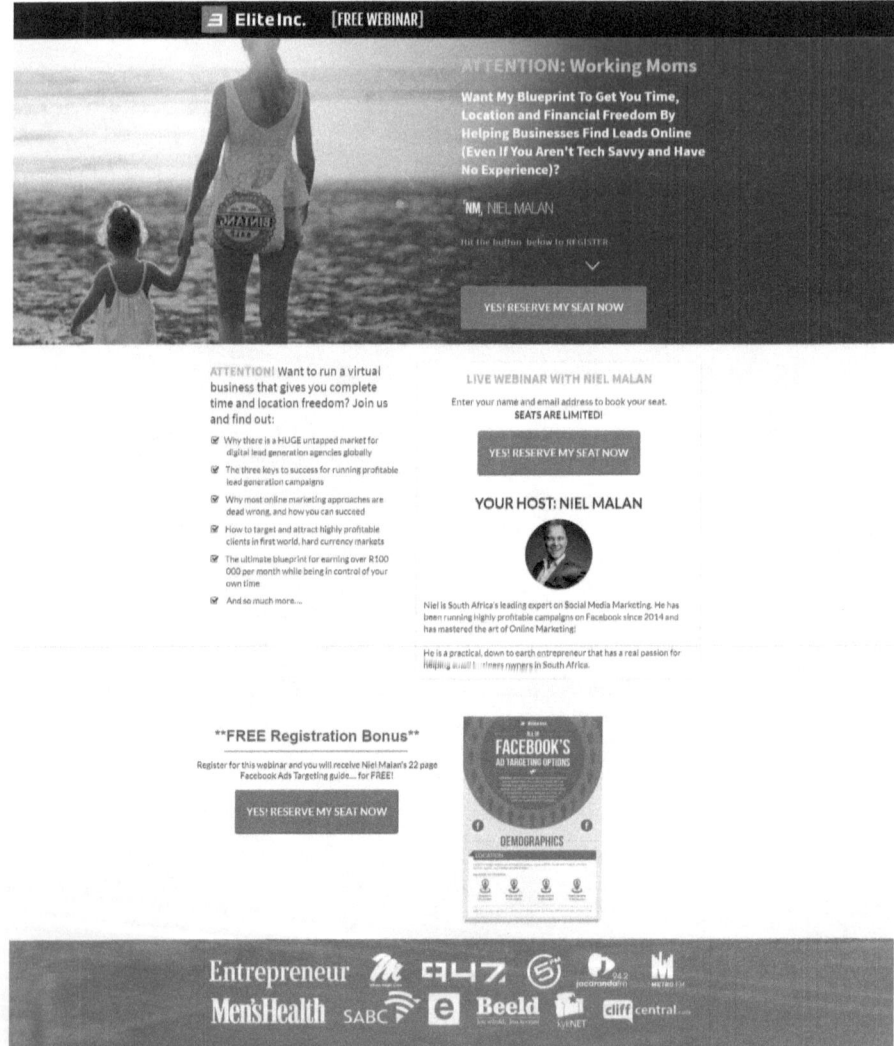

When the prospect clicks an ad, they want to know more. Whether it's a blog article, testimonial video, or product sales page, tell a story that gets them curious enough to take the *next* step—a landing page.

Everything you need to know about designing and managing landing pages, you'll learn in the context of the Funnel Strategy in Chapter 6.

For the purposes of your high ROI Messaging Strategy, all you need to know about landing pages right now is what to *put* on them.

For example, if I direct people to an article about learning digital marketing with a Facebook ad, I want readers to get curious about which program they should join. Then at the end of the article, I send them to my Agency FastTrack product page.

So now you know. Ads are not intended to create a sale instantly, they're meant to move prospects from one stage of awareness to the next. Now let's take a look at what it takes to grab attention and get that click, one piece at a time.

Headlines and Ad Copy—hook, line, and sale.

When you were in school and the teacher asked you to solve a math problem, what did you do? You used a **formula**. Every time you needed to figure out that unknown side of a triangle, you used the Pythagorean theorem. It worked every time.

The same is true of winning ad headlines. They follow one of many proven formulas that either ask a question, tell a story, or make a statement to "hook" prospects so the rest of the ad can reel them in.

Here are my top three highest converting headline formulas. They've worked for me, my clients, and students of Agency FastTrack time after time in industry after industry. Just like you wrote down those maths formulas on an index card to consult during a test, keep these three formulas near your computer so you're always ready to earn those ad clicks:

- **How to** [achieve specific result] **without** [experiencing side effect]
    - **Example:** "How to get rid of belly fat without eating vegetables for breakfast"
- **How do I** [enjoy extraordinary benefit] **from** [something ordinary]?
    - **Example:** "How do I make money from my Facebook Business Page?"
- **FREE** [content] **on how to** [achieve extraordinary result]
    - **Example:** "FREE webinar on how to start a profitable social media agency"

The fun doesn't end there. In 2017, BuzzSumo, an online research platform, reviewed over one hundred million headlines to determine which formulas work best...and least.[4] According to BuzzSumo, the internet's **best performing headline formulas** are:

1. ...will make you...
2. This is why...
3. Can we guess...
4. ...only X in...
5. ...the reason is...
6. ...are freaking out...
7. # stunning photos...
8. ...tears of joy.
9. ...is what happens...
10. ...make you cry.

Wow! A LOT of emotions make that list—exactly what we'd expect to see since humans respond to stories. At the very bottom of BuzzSumo's list are *fact*-based headlines.[5] These top ten **worst performing headline formulas** are:

1. ...control of your...
2. ...your own business.
3. ...work for you.
4. The introduction of...
5. What's new in...
6. Could you be...
7. The effect of...
8. # simple tips...
9. ...best for you.
10. The nature of...

In the race to win customers away from the competition, formulas are your agency's high performance fuel. But what goes *inside* a formula determines how much traction your messaging gets on the road to the sale.

Fortunately, you've got your Avatar. The better you understand what makes your client's Avatar tick, the easier it is to write dynamite messages. If you can use the *actual words* your Avatar uses to describe their problem, look for a solution, and choose the right product, you're able to enter the conversation already going on inside their heads and persuade them to buy.

The fastest way to uncover an audience's actual words is to borrow a little-known market research hack from marketing legend Jay Abraham—whose ads have generated over nine *billion dollars* in revenue.[6,7]

Go to Amazon.com and type your client's subject matter in the search box. For example, I'd type "starting a digital marketing agency" for Agency FastTrack.

Why books? Because book buyers sit right on the edge of curiosity and commitment. Readers—your clients' future customers—are curious enough about an industry to pay twenty bucks for a book, but not quite committed enough to spend hundreds or thousands on a solution...*yet*.

To figure out what "specific result" your Avatar wants to achieve, what "side effect" they're worried about, and what "extraordinary benefit" they desire, scan those books like there's no tomorrow!

Start with the top ten bestselling books in your subject matter category. Copy and paste the book titles, subtitles, and book description into a "headline and copy ideas" document. These words and phrases are the results and benefits people *pay for* to learn all about your client's product.

Then, move on to the verified reader reviews. Pay special attention to the four, three, and two-star reviews, which tend to be more balanced feedback where people describe what they loved, what they hated, and what made them want more.

If I'm reading reviews for *The Ultimate Guide to Starting a Digital Agency* and spot a three-star rating where the reviewers says, "I've gone through the theory but still don't know how to put it into practice," I've hit **gold**. When one person admits something, thousands think it.

I immediately copy and paste this insight in my "headline and copy ideas" document for Agency FastTrack (You have one for each client, right?). That way, I'll be able to address my Avatar's worry about starting a digital agency in my Avatar's own words!

My next headline might read something like, "The step-by-step practical blueprint for starting a digital agency." In this example, I communicate the specific results that going through Agency FastTrack offers while taking a top, real world concern off the table. After reading this copy, my customer realizes they can have their cake and eat it too...all because I "borrowed" their own words! Congratulations, you've found the shortcut to copywriting mastery.

Images—no, attractive young females aren't enough.

Whenever I've spoken with small business owners from around the world about images for their Facebook ads, sex appeal *always* comes up at some point.

"Can't we just use a stock photo of a hot woman looking at the camera?"

No. The job of an ad's image is to complement the copy, *not* to get people complimenting the model's attractiveness! Amateur or professional photography matters a lot less than the characteristics of the subject. Look at your client's Avatar. Is she a forty year-old married mother who wants to try something new with her hair? If your client is a local salon, have one of the hairdressers snap a quick photo of a forty year-old married mother who is trying something new with her hair—bleached, braids, buzzed on one side, whatever.

If your client's product or service is difficult (or impossible) for a customer to model, showcase one of their most popular or unique products. Take the subscription service, The Gin Box for example. Each package includes one of the top small-batch gins, along with products and recipes to create your very own craft gin experience in your kitchen.

As you might imagine, The Gin Box advertisements are quite beautiful. One promotional image neatly arranges the box and its content on an ocean pier's ledge. A blurry yet striking blue sky and sandy shoreline appear in the background [8]. You see yourself there, enjoying the refreshments. It's a story, and *you're* the main character.

CHAPTER 5 - YOUR SECOND HIGH ROI STRATEGY: MESSAGING

Whether your clients sell beverage products or hairdressing services, you can also use Facebook's Canvas feature to display multiple photos in a single ad so prospects can scroll your clients' top three, five, or ten selling points in a matter of seconds!

Videos—and why they're worth a thousand pictures.

As our social media attention spans get shorter and shorter, marketers have fewer and fewer *tenths* of a second to engage prospects. That's why videos are so critical to any high ROI campaign: once you get someone watching, chances are, they *keep* watching—and reading.

Yes, *reading*. Crazy as it is, eighty-five percent of all Facebook video ads online are watched on Facebook's default audio mode—mute.[9] If you're going to leverage the power of visual marketing for your clients, put "create captions" at the top of your video ad campaign to-do list.

Then we have to plan the video's actual content. When Agency Fast-Track students ask me, "What's the ideal length for a video?" I tell them the truth:

"There is none!"

Let the content determine the length. If I'm planning on running an Agency FastTrack video ad to "A" stage prospects—people who are already familiar with how starting a digital agency can get you to the location, time, and freedom goals you crave—I need to position Agency FastTrack as the most comprehensive, proven, and effective way to do so. A fifteen-second or even sixty-second video wouldn't be long enough. That's not enough time to tell the story of Agency FastTrack. Facebook does prefer that advertisers publish short videos, but they prefer videos *people actually watch* even more! So if my video ran five, seven, or ten minutes, I'd have no problem. Neither would Facebook—as long as people watch it.

So quality content is key. So is quality *style*. After investing several hundred thousand dollars in video ads for my own business, I've seen four specific production styles that keep people watching long past the first few curiosity-provoking seconds.

Video style one: Someone talks live to the camera. There are no props or presentation slides. This works really well if your speaker is lively, approachable, and comfortable in front of a camera.

Video style two: A talking head is joined on screen by images, slides, or a mind map.

Video style three: An explainer video. These are best done as digital whiteboard drawings or animated stories that "explain" the story.

Video style four: A narrated video. It's the least preferred type of video because only images, slides, or diagrams are visible.

What *is* important in video is that the pacing be fast. To excel at video ads, your actor (the business owner) must up their enthusiasm and speak very, very quickly. It will *feel* over the top—but it will *look* normal. You need a *lot* of energy to get people's attention!

When it comes to structuring your video, I recommend a five second opening "hook." Here, you either get people watching or you don't. To begin a video, lots of movement helps. Make people curious. For example, if you have a whiteboard behind you, stand and point at the content. You could also start with the strongest benefit of your product. For example, I could start an Agency FastTrack video by saying,

"The complete blueprint for starting and running a digital agency." If my Avatar is interested, they're going to watch. I could also start with a compelling question like, "What is the best business opportunity right now?" Put as much thought into those first five seconds as you do the remaining minutes.

For the video content, combine education, entertainment, and inspiration. Say something like, "Guys, I've got something incredible to tell you that you're gonna love…" or say, "In this video, I'm going to tell you a secret…" You want people feeling hopeful, not fearful. I could also say, "If you've been struggling with getting work/life balance, I've got the solution for you…" Close out your videos with a call-to-action. It's as simple as saying, "Click the link below."

To shoot these videos, all you need is a smartphone, a tripod, and a light. Smartphones shoot near-professional quality videos, so if your clients have a phone, they have what Hollywood film producers didn't have barely a decade ago. In my experience, the ideal number of video takes is ten. It's easier to shoot great videos than most agency owners think, which is why they don't offer to help their clients do it. Another advantage for you!

The best part about video advertising is that you don't have to do it right the first time! On the day of a shoot, when your client's pulse is pounding hard enough to give them a migraine, calm their nerves. Tell them, "We'll do ten takes total. For the first two or three takes, I want you to be terrible!"

They'll laugh, take a deep breath, and release that self-imposed pressure to get it right on the first take. They'll probably feel comfortable on camera right around the fourth or fifth take. Once you see them getting into a groove, pause in between takes and offer constructive feedback on what you'd like them to do or say differently next time. When you reach the ninth or tenth take, they'll look like a natural on camera!

I've had mom and pop business owners go from stage fright to stage presence in the space of an hour because we committed to ten video takes. So have Agency FastTrack students with their clients. And so can you.

Landing pages—so much more than one-page websites.

Now that your prospect has clicked on your ad (congratulations!), be it an image or video ad, you have the opportunity to put a message in front of them. One that will get them all excited about finding a solution, choosing the *right* solution, or purchasing your client's solution—depending on their R.E.A.D.Y. stage.

Since Chapter 6 is your Funnel Strategy how-to manual in which landing pages are the main lesson, I am going to briefly touch on the most commonly used—but least effective—type of page to which advertisers drive traffic: the article landing page.

If you've done your job right (and you have), prospects clicked your client's ad because you hooked them with your headline and aroused their curiosity with the ad's content. Great job!

For most small businesses, blog articles are an afterthought. They miss the fact that every piece of content should have a single objective. For example, if I'm writing an article on the best business opportunity to take advantage of right now, the first thing my Avatar needs to buy into is that starting and running a digital agency is *the* answer. Investing in a franchise for instance, is not the way to go.

Before anything else happens, know your objective: to move your Avatar from their current R.E.A.D.Y. stage to the next.

So how do you even begin going about writing an article or a blog?

Pretty simple, actually. When you do research for an article, find substantiating research from professional sources and be sure to cite the links. The more credible your information sources are, the more believable your claims. If I wrote an article which claimed, "Starting a digital agency is the best because it's so popular!" I'd have zero credibility and probably close to zero buyers.

A great way to compile trusted sources is to look up your subject matter on Wikipedia and look at their citations section. Which professional sources are cited? Use those!

Once you've got the research you need to prove your point, map out the article itself. If the destination is your Avatar getting closer to purchasing, then the journey is every turn you have them take to get there.

Start with a **one-paragraph overview**, for example. "So you want time, location, and financial freedom? What are your options? There are thousands of books out there with regards to the many types of opportunities that can supposedly give you that freedom, and consumers are confused. Is there credible research which shows one avenue works better than others?"

Next, position your topic in its proper **context** for people who aren't familiar. "A lot of people are talking about getting time, location, and financial freedom. But is it really possible?"

Once people understand where your article is going, focus on the **top five key insights** from your research.

"I'm guessing this isn't the first article you've read about how to start your own business. I'm not going to lie, the internet is full of them. It seems as though everyone who's ever even taught about breaking out on their own has, at some point, written an article about their experience.

"But the question I want to ask you today is this: After reading some of these articles, how is anyone even remotely inspired to go out and start their own business? Because they all seem to follow the same formula. They all talk about the importance of assessing your finances, writing business plans, getting all the legal stuff drawn up, finding suitable premises....it's daunting to say the least"

I'm not presenting opinions, and I'm not manipulating data to pretend something is true when it isn't.

Once you've laid out your key insights, **summarize the argument** you've just presented. For my example, that might be: "I'm certainly not suggesting there's anything wrong with any of the advice you might have watched or read before today. What I am asking, though, is this:

Is it the best advice for you? Is it going to give you the financial freedom you want? And will it enable you to live and work location free?

"If not, then perhaps it's time to think a little outside the box. Hell, why not just go all in and throw the box away? Because you don't just want to start any old business. You want to start one that actually makes you money. Serious money. Without having to work one hundred hours a week, without chaining yourself to your desk, and without having to invest your life savings into a venture that only might work.

"Because let's face it. Over eighty percent of new businesses fail within the first three years. It's a frightening statistic, and one you definitely don't want to be part of. And you don't have to. Not if you choose a business with virtually unlimited growth potential. One that not only makes money for you, but for your clients as well. And we all know that clients who make money doing what you tell them to are more than happy to keep paying you!"

That opens the door for me to introduce that easy way—Agency FastTrack.

"If you want to get the step-by-step blueprint on how to earn ten thousand dollars in a month in retainers, then join the thousands of students that have taken their destiny into their own hands and joined Agency FastTrack. Click here." Then that link drives readers to the Agency FastTrack product page.

Once you've got all the elements of a winning ad, you're ready for the **second aspect of the Messaging Strategy: stage-specific ads**.

As you know, not every ad is intended to create a sale, but every ad *is* intended to make prospects *closer* to a sale. That's why stage-specific messaging matters. For example, a great Agency FastTrack ad headline is *only* great if it speaks to the current level of a customer's awareness. Your headline needs to address the question that's most relevant in their mind *right now*. I don't talk about starting a digital agency in my ads to unaware customers because they don't understand the relationship between starting a digital agency and time, financial, and location freedom. I can think of no better way to teach stage-specific messaging than showing you real-life examples.

CHAPTER 5 - YOUR SECOND HIGH ROI STRATEGY: MESSAGING

Elite Inc
Sponsored

Are you tired of missing out on time with your kids because you're working all the time?

It's tough being a working Mom. You're torn between needing to do a good job for your boss, but wanting to be there for your children. You miss out on so many events in their lives - moments you'll never get back - but what can you do? You have to work to help support their lifestyle.

It's got to the point where you're not sure who's winning - your guilt or your exhaustion. One thing's for sure though: It's not your kids.

But it's not your fault...

What if there was a way you could earn enough to secure a comfortable lifestyle for your family, while still being able to watch your children play sport, or collect that award? What if you could choose your own hours, work location free, and enjoy a work-life balance you never dared dreamed was possible?

You can, and I'm going to show you how.

Stop letting someone else dictate how you earn an income! I can show you how to gain financial freedom and take control of your own destiny. Today.

https://bit.ly/2EmEF0n

[BLOG] UNLOCK YOUR FINANCIAL FUTURE AND TAKE BACK YOUR LIFE
Gain Financial Freedom And Take Control Of Your Destiny With...
HTTPS://WWW.ELITEINC.COM/CATEGORY/BLOG/

537   257 Comments   117 Shares

Elite Inc — Sponsored · Like Page

🙁 Are you still feeling guilty about missing out on time with your kids?

We know you want the best for your kids, which is why you work so hard to provide the best possible lifestyle for them.

But do you know what else we know? You don't want to give up your job because, let's face it, you love the challenge or worse yet, you're afraid of the financial impact it will have on your family...But at the end of the day, your kids don't want more things, they want more you.

Agree? ✓✓✓

But is that elusive laptop lifestyle really in reach? Or is it just a pipe dream someone made up to make you feel more guilty?

The thing is, that dream can become a reality – you just need to know what to do...

So, if you're ready to change your life, live and work location free, and enjoy unparalleled financial freedom, I want to share my blueprint with you! For FREE!

https://bit.ly/2EmEF0n

[BLOG] HERE'S HOW YOU COULD SOON BE LIVING THE LAPTOP LIFESTYLE
Want My Blueprint To Get Time, Location And Financial Freedom...
HTTPS://WWW.ELITEINC.COM/CATEGORY/BLOG/ — Sign Up

👍❤ 276   221 Comments   147 Shares

👍 Like   💬 Comment   ➤ Share

CHAPTER 5 - YOUR SECOND HIGH ROI STRATEGY: MESSAGING

Sending the right message at the right time *is* a science, but it's a simple science. When you know how customers think at each of the Five R.E.A.D.Y. stages, you can easily put the exact right message in front of them at exactly the right time. Small business owners will do anything to find someone who knows how to do this. They'll be curious how you run stage one ads to stage one customers, stage two ads to stage two customers, and so forth, but all they'll *really* want to know is whether you can turn a hundred bucks into three hundred.

You, on the other hand, must be able to answer these questions. How *do* you put stage one ads in front of prospects at the first stage of awareness? You can't actually advertise to *only* stage one customers, right? Or can you? That's a question answered by the Funnel.

CHAPTER 6

YOUR THIRD HIGH ROI STRATEGY: FUNNELS

On average, what percentage of website visitors do you think buy on the spot?

Twenty percent? Ten percent? Five percent?

How about...**2.35 percent**.[1]

That's a problem—let's have a look at the math.

Let's say a local salon runs Google PPC ads to the home page of their website. At the cost of $1 per click, the salon gets two new customers for a hundred bucks. Since the average woman's haircut is $43, the salon loses money on this straight-to-the-website ad campaign—and their agency loses them as a client. **That's a problem**.

But there *is* a solution. Since you know about the Five Stage of R.E.A.D.Y., you probably know why these homepage conversion rates are so low. Most small business websites are written for fifth stage clients, that three percent of people who intend to make a purchase. Small business websites feature their product or service (solution), and most incoming traffic know they need it. It's hand-in-glove.

Still, it's a very, very small glove. Your clients are going to rely on your digital agency to create customers for them out of the ninety-seven percent, the other stages of R.E.A.D.Y. If you're going to do that—and you *will*, I promise!—you need something better than clicks to a website. **You need a Funnel.**

As you read in the last chapter, Funnels are more than a one-page website with a free offer, a one-time coupon, or a special deal—they're ALL of those and then some! I think of Funnels as a low-risk, low-friction relationship with potential customers. One that helps them get to know a business, like a business, and trust a business to the point that they're ready to buy.

To that end, your **Funnel Strategy** is a strategic, systematic process to turn stage one "really unaware" customers into stage two "problem educated" customers, stage two customers into stage three "solution aware" customers, stage three customers into stage four "deciding" customers, and finally, to turn stage four customers into stage five "yes" customers.

Most importantly, Funnels are your structured way to run stage one specific messages to stage one customers, stage two specific messages to stage two customers, and so on. Naturally, like the usual small business website, Funnels are technology-dependent. But because tech changes so often, this chapter will remain agnostic on the question of which Funnel software you should use. (However, to see my most up to date software recommendation, go to EliteInc.com/AgencyBookResources.)

No matter which Funnel software you choose, your **Funnel Strategy objectives** are the same. You and your client both know a Funnel is working when these five things happen consistently:

1. Your Funnel drives traffic from **ads** to **landing pages**.
2. The landing page makes an irresistible **offer**.
3. The customer redeems the offer, becoming a **lead**.
4. You systematically convert that lead into a **customer**.
5. Your **relationship** ascends, and the customer buys again.

Notice something about these five steps? They correspond to each of the Five Stages of R.E.A.D.Y.! So every time a person takes action—clicks the ad, reads about the offer, accepts the offer, etc., etc.—they are moving themselves from one R.E.A.D.Y. stage to the next of their own volition! That's why Messaging Strategy matters so much more than Funnels—get the stage-specific content right, and your audience naturally moves themselves through each stage towards purchase. Is it any wonder Funnels convert anywhere from ten percent to fifty percent of traffic into customers, compared to a website's two percent average? No other marketing strategy produces the high ROI that Funnels do, which makes them indispensable.

Let me give you an example of these Five Funnel Strategy steps from a real life business—my mom's. She's a fantastic clinical psychologist in Cape Town, South Africa. First, she runs a simple ad for people looking for a psychologist in Cape Town. When they land on her landing page, they see an offer for a free Skype consultation, or an offer to download a free worksheet called "Five Tips to Get Relief from Depression without Medication." Or perhaps she has an article people can read entitled, "Five Healthy Ways to Grieve the Loss of a Loved One." Once people redeem her offer, a certain percentage will actually buy a one-off consultation to try her out. You typically don't buy a series of appointments since you want to test drive the experience. But once people enjoy benefits from the first consultation and like it, she offers six, twelve, or twenty session packages, or three to six months of psychotherapy or psychoanalysis sessions to help them long-term.

That's how a relationship forms through a Funnel. Let me give you another example—a dentist. Let's say someone is Googling around for a dentist in New York City (someone probably is right this very second!). They see a dentist's ad and click on their landing page, where they see an offer for a free teeth cleaning.

"Wow! I don't have to pay for a teeth cleaning *and* I get to test drive this new dentist? Fantastic!"

So the lead puts their information in the landing page form and schedules their free cleaning. If the dentist is clever—and they are because they're your client in this example—when the patient comes in for their appointment, they turn a free appointment into that first sale.

"You've got plaque and a cavity," the dentist tells his new patient, who decides to book another appointment on the spot to deal with the cavity. Then at the next appointment, the dentist offers teeth whitening, dental veneers, implants, and other more expensive procedures. As a result, the dentist has a long-term customer who returns whenever they need dental care.

Not every industry is that easy to move customers from ad traffic to long-term relationship. What about traditionally "once-off" businesses, like a real estate agent?

In that case, you're not going to think about selling multiple products or services at first, you're going to think about the *progression* of the relationship. Let's say someone is looking for a beautiful beach house in San Diego, California. They see an ad with the headline, "The Ultimate San Diego Home Buyers' Guide." They click on the ad, visit the landing page, and see a free offer for an ebook entitled *Seven Things You Need to Know Before Buying Property in San Diego.* People fill out the form to claim the offer, and the San Diego based real estate agent calls them the next day and says, "Hi! It looks like you're interested in buying a home in San Diego because you downloaded my free guide. I have a process that I use to help people identify the ideal property for them. I'd like to set up a free one hour consultation with you, where I'll guide you through a worksheet and identify the type of property that best fits your needs."

That consultation replaces the first sale because it's the first face-to-face experience. At that appointment, the agent builds rapport with the client and shows them several properties which fit their needs—one of which they decide to buy. If this client is a high net-worth person who might be interested in real estate investment opportunities, the real estate agent can create a premium San Diego property investment training to sell to her client. Long-term relationship, established!

To serve your clients properly, whether they're service providers or a mom and pop shop that sells products, you're going to follow the same Funnel Strategy steps in these examples. That said, there is no one-size-fits-everybody Funnel ad, landing page, offer, or first product. Your job isn't to tell your clients what box their business fits into. It's to help them determine what each step of a Funnel should look like, based on their Avatar and what their future customers need to know at each stage of awareness.

Just as you met with your clients to complete the Avatar worksheet, you're going to schedule a meeting to talk Funnels. Because the first action a prospect takes after clicking an ad is responding to a business' offer (or not), start there with your clients. Get clarity about their specific offer.

A great offer provides a strong incentive to learn more, like the Buyers' Guide example, which is easy to say yes to. The fewer hurdles you ask a customer to jump over, the better, so make your offer easy to redeem. Exclusive white papers, useful checklists, or handy cheat sheets in exchange for a prospect's name and email are fair.

Your offer also has to position your client favorably. Credibility and expertise matter, so your landing page copy should include a brief section that gives specific reasons why they're a reputable company, such as awards or testimonials.

Your offer should also educate your client's customers, making them aware of their problem, the potential solutions, and *your client's* solution. When I ran Facebook ads for my business coaching services several years ago, I offered my business owner prospects a free sales training session for their entire sales staff. They couldn't say no! When I got in front of those sales teams, explained the top mistakes salespeople make, and explained my unique sales process, over *half* of the businesses hired my company before I left!

Ideally, your offer creates a powerful first impression and proves its value. It's an opportunity for your prospects to test drive a business, whether it's a free Skype consultation, a free downloadable guide, or a free training. Then, like my earlier dentist example, that offer moves a prospect right into the first purchase. From there, that first purchase, usually a lower-priced product or service so they can test drive the business further, leads up the value ladder to higher priced products or services. (In most cases, your offer appears on a landing page.)

DIGITAL AGENCY FASTTRACK

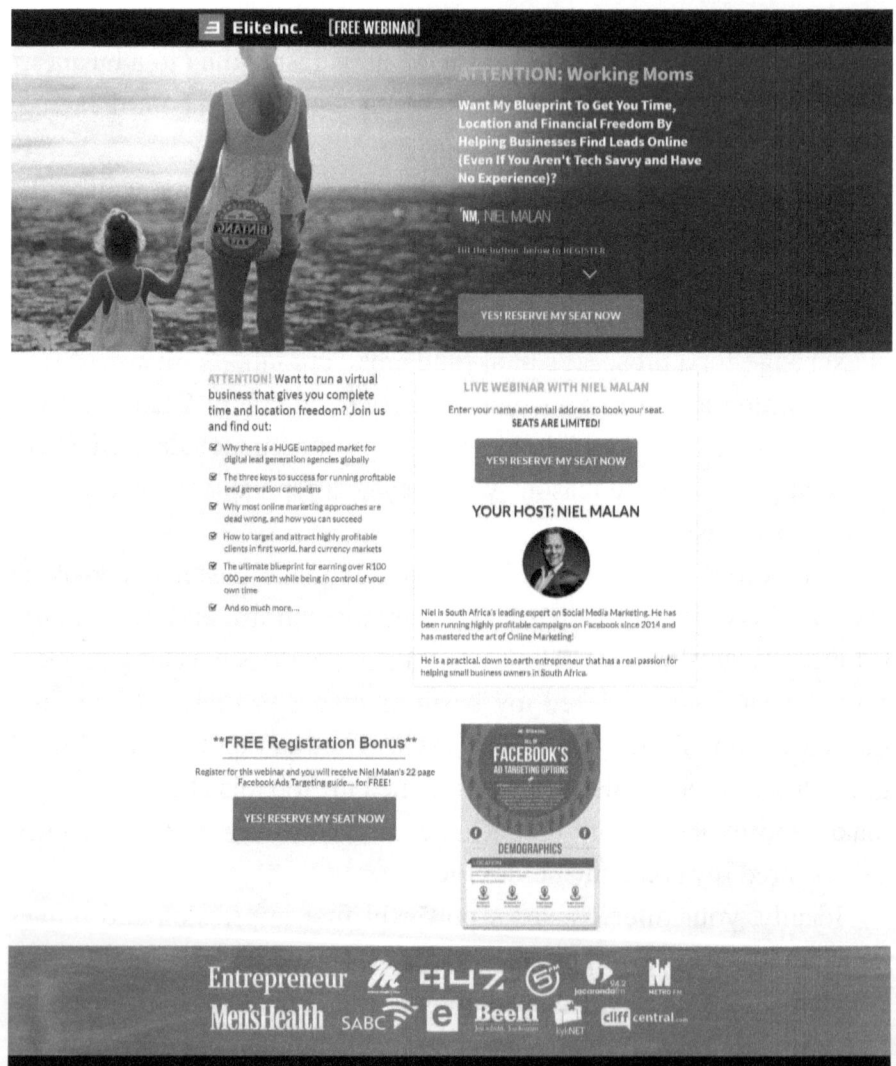

Once you help your client figure out what offer most excites their Avatar, it's your job to create a corresponding ad and landing page. You know all about winning messages thanks to Chapter 5, so let's have a look at the secrets of high-converting landing pages. This way, the traffic your clients are paying for, consistently produces ROI!

In many ways, landing pages are the opposite of a business website home page. Website home pages have general information about a business and feature multiple calls-to-action (newsletter signup, request a quote, etc.). But a landing page shows *only* information pertinent to the offer, and therefore shows only *one* call-to-action.

If for some reason you are not using a Funnel software, you can still create a Funnel-style landing page. All you have to do is publish a web page like you normally would on the website, then disable the menu and navigation options and remove any social media buttons. That way, all traffic incoming to the website sees no distractions. Their attention is completely on your client's *one* offer and the *one* way they can accept, sign up, or buy it.

Since most Funnel software includes both a built-in contacts database (called a "Customer Relationship Management" platform, or CRM) and email autoresponder software, you'll need to integrate your makeshift landing page call-to-action form with your own CRM. Without a place to store all the information you're collecting from your clients' leads, your Funnel is toast! Again, tech changes often, so check out EliteInc.com/AgencyBookResources to see which Funnel software, CRM, and email autoresponder software I recommend.

Whether you buy a Funnel software license or design one from scratch, there's a lot that goes into an effective Funnel! Each aspect has to work together to create a sale, from the ad, to the landing page, to the offer, to the first sale, and beyond. Technology enables a Funnel to work, so I don't want you leaving this chapter without knowing *exactly* how to *build* one for your first (or next) client. And the best way to learn anything is by **example**.

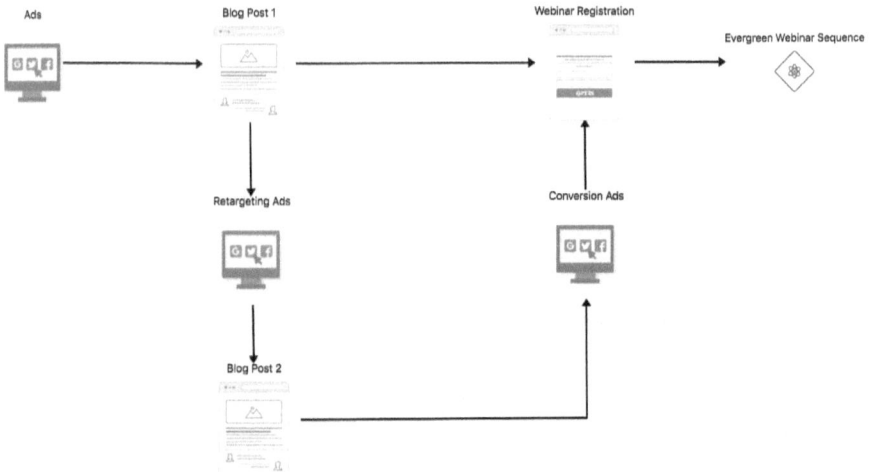

You've covered all of the strategies—Audience, Messaging, Funnel. You know how to build a client's business up with a high ROI service. But what about *your* business, the digital agency?

Over the next several chapters, I'm going to show you how to grow your business from the ground up, then scale it to a six-figure or even seven-figure enterprise. And like any business, you don't *have* a business without customers.

So let me show you how to find them.

CHAPTER 7

MARKETING THE MARKETER: FINDING CLIENTS FOR YOUR AGENCY

Several years ago, I attended an internet marketing conference in the States. During a breakout session, digital agency owners fielded questions from aspiring entrepreneurs in the audience.

One particularly excited audience member said, "I just started my web agency. How should I go about getting my first few clients?"

The four panelists exchanged awkward looks with each other.

"To be honest, we're still figuring that one out for ourselves." He laughed. "It's tough out here, you know? We struggled to find good clients early on, too. You just have to try a few different strategies and see what works."

The audience member looked like a four year-old whose ice cream fell off his cone.

Honestly, I felt worse for the panelist. It's your job to advertise other companies online, but you can't advertise yourself? What does that tell your clients?

Like the panelist with his ridiculous answer, most agency owners approach marketing their companies all wrong. If I'd been on that panel, I would've said *exactly* what I'm telling you now:

Marketing your agency is easy. It's *so* easy, in fact, that you only have to do it once.

The fact is, once you've got the skills to generate ROI for your very first clients, getting more clients won't be hard. The word-of-mouth marketing your clients do on your behalf works better than any campaign. They won't be able to shut up about the results your Funnels bring them—daily inquiries, daily leads, daily sales. And because you have a long-term mutually rewarding relationship with your clients, you'll need *fewer* clients than your competitors, who build a small business website here and write Facebook ad copy there.

The key is those very first clients, the first three to five small business owners willing to take your services for a test drive. That's why marketing your agency is a one-time stage in your business' growth, no more than three to six months, period. So you have this initial thrust where you *do* put a lot of effort into finding and winning those first few clients so you never have to again (unless you want to).

Of course, you want your first client batch to be *high quality*. Unlike our panelist friend, you don't want to take on *any* client who comes along simply because you're just starting out. If a client's product is not an easy sell, guess what? You won't sell it, and you'll break your confidence. And if a client hassles you on pricing, they'll likely take up most of your time and suck the life out of you, preventing you from going out and getting quality, new clients.

From the very beginning, you want to discern which leads to accept as clients and which to reject, and the only way you *get* to discern is to generate a massive flow of leads. Ideally, you want three to five leads for every client. That way, you can literally pick and choose the best opportunities for your agency. In Chapter 8, we'll have a look at your lead vetting criteria. For now, adopt the mindset that you *should* vet leads, not just accept any small business into your agency.

So, how do you get aggressive with business development and generate a ton of inquiries to choose from?

Be your own best client.

Just as you're going to build Funnels for your clients, build them for yourself! The best position you can be in is the position you put your

CHAPTER 7 - MARKETING THE MARKETER: FINDING CLIENTS FOR YOUR AGENCY

own clients in—having advertising campaigns that send you a rush of leads whenever you feel like turning on the tap.

And instead of just "doing marketing," you're going to build a marketing *system*. You don't do one-off projects for your clients right from the get-go, so don't create one-off advertising campaigns for yourself. Think long-term. In Chapter 10, I'm going to teach you how to scale your agency when the time feels right. That's why, even if you technically don't *want* a system, you may very well need one. Because without a system, you're doing things manually. Manual work takes a lot of effort, memory, and focus, all of which are in short supply when you're booked solid.

Your marketing system has three building blocks—your Virtual Assistant, your KPIs dashboard, and marketing strategies.

As soon as you can afford your first hire, you'll want to hire a Virtual Assistant. Not for administrative tasks, bookkeeping, or doing your laundry, but for marketing and only marketing. Even if your new agency budget only allows for two or three hours a week for a few bucks an hour, start there! Without a VA, your focus is split between your business and those of your clients. So every week, schedule a call with your Virtual Assistant to answer any questions they might have about managing your dashboard or following through on your strategies. (See EliteInc.com/AgencyBookResources for my latest VA hiring recommendations.)

Now, speaking of your dashboard, your VA can create something as simple as a spreadsheet, or you can use a premium marketing dashboard software. (See EliteInc.com/AgencyBookResources for my dashboard recommendations.) You want to track these metrics on your dashboard: Leads In, Leads in Progress, and Deals Won. What doesn't get measured, doesn't get managed. And if you can't manage the leads you're getting, you won't be able to easily improve your closing rate.

For example, let's say you get seven leads next month, two of which become clients. If your goal is four new clients per month for the next three months, you need to generate forteen leads per month on average.

So, how do you actually *get* those leads in the first place? In Agency FastTrack, I teach up and coming agency owners thirty-five different ways for newbies to get clients, but here are the **Top Fifteen** I see students coming back to over and over as they grow from two or three clients to twenty to thirty clients.

That said, whenever I talk about the best ways to find clients, whether it's on a webinar or in a blog post, a ton of aspiring agency owners write in and ask me the same few questions:

"I'd love to be able to run a virtual business from anywhere in the world and provide really cool digital marketing services to my clients. But there's a problem—I'm a virgin! Do I first get clients, and then develop my skills through those clients? Or do I first develop the skills and then get clients?"

A real chicken and egg situation, isn't it? Yes, I can teach you everything you need to *know* about running a high ROI digital agency (hence this book), but you can't *develop* the skills you need unless you're using them.

Confusing, isn't it? Let's solve this problem with **Practice Clients**, the first of my fifteen strategies.

Your practice clients are one email, one message, one chat away. Approach any small business owner you know—your family, your Facebook friends, your LinkedIn connections, your email contacts, your extended network—with a simple, non-threatening offer, "I'm reading this book about generating leads off Facebook and Google, and I need to practice on someone. If you're interested in getting more clients, I will provide my services to you for free for the next two to three months. I'm going to tell you exactly what I do as we test the strategies from the book. All I want you to do is to commit to a small ad spend of between $250 and $500 per month, but there's no obligation to continue with me afterwards."

Welcome to the easiest sale you're ever going to make! The practice clients strategy is the ideal departure point for total beginners because it's virtually risk-free. You're starting with people who already know you, like you, and trust you. The less nervous you are, the less likely you are to screw up, and the more likely you are to impress your two or three practice clients with tangible results.

So now, you've got the skills you need to generate leads for a business in real life. Eventually, you'll want to deploy your own Funnel to get those leads and turn them into clients. For your agency's first Funnel to work, you're going to need some case studies and testimonials—proof you know your stuff.

That's where the **second strategy** comes in, the **Eager Student Approach**. Advertising expert Dan Henry taught me this strategy, and it works like this:

Start by picking a niche. One niche, any niche; it doesn't matter what. It could be doctors, dentists, chiropractors, yoga studio practitioners, or real estate agents. You want to go for one industry so you can master high ROI lead generation and customer acquisition with one business in that niche, then take that Funnel to ten other businesses in that industry in different parts of the world and replicate that success. For example, you can have one client in Singapore, another in London, and another in New Zealand, but they're all dentists. If you can make money for a dentist in New York, then you can make money for a dentist in Australia.

Let's say you want to service dentists. Before you go big and market your agency to dentists, you need to run campaigns for two or three dentists who will give you that precious testimonial. I simply can't exaggerate how important it is for you to have a written review on your website like, "This person knows how to generate leads for dentists."

Similar to the first strategy, you're going to go digging for practice clients, except in a niche-specific place. But just like your first two or three practice clients, your eager students won't be that hard to find in Facebook groups, LinkedIn groups, or online forums specifically for your niche.

For example, when I search "Dentists" on Facebook and narrow my search results to show only "Groups," I see dozens of groups I can request to join. Once approved, you'll post a very simple message to everyone that goes, "Hey guys, I just finished this book that shows how to drive leads from platforms like Facebook and Google. I've decided to take on two or three dentists for free to practice my skills, and all I want in return is a written testimonial if I succeed. Please let me know if you're interested, and we can schedule a call."

Boom! You've exposed thousands and thousands and thousands of people in your niche to your business without spending a cent. Now, you will get a thousand replies, but all you want are two or three dentists to say, "Okay, that sounds pretty cool. Let's get something on the calendar."

What's nice about the first two strategies is your honesty. You don't have to pretend to be an expert. The pressure's off, and you now have the opportunity to get really, *really* good—and to take advantage of my **third strategy**, the **Pixel Helper**.

Let's say you're passionate about dentistry, so you want to get dentists to pay you between $1,500 and $3,500 per month to provide your services. Before you talk about pixels, you're going to find dentists in expensive cities all around the world.

A few years back, I cracked a tooth while traveling to New York City on business. It cost me a fortune to fix! Being a dentist is very profitable in New York City, so that's a good place to start. Just go to Google and type "dentist New York." Google will then show you ten dentist ads and ten first page search results.

Now you want to find out how many of these guys are advertising on Facebook (or not). You'll recall from Chapter 1 the Tracking Pixel tool I recommended—a free browser extension to see whether or not a website has a Pixel to track all website visitors all across the internet.

Use the Pixel Helper tool to check which dentist websites have a Pixel and which do not. For the ones that do, chances are they've got an agency already helping them advertise on Facebook, so I may not want to contact them.

When you *do* find a dentist without a Pixel, do a traffic analysis to see if they get enough web traffic to make retargeting their traffic with Facebook ads worthwhile. Certain internet browsers offer free plugins that allow you to run these analyses in less than thirty seconds. (Check out EliteInc.com/AgencyBookResources for my latest traffic analyzer recommendations.)

When I followed these steps in preparation for this book, I found a dentist on Wall Street who gets 1,500 website visits every single month,

CHAPTER 7 - MARKETING THE MARKETER: FINDING CLIENTS FOR YOUR AGENCY

yet they're not following them back to Facebook and running retargeting ads.

Boom, you've got a wonderful opportunity. Reach out to your Pixel-less dentist offices and say, "Hey, who runs your marketing?"

When they give you that person's name, get ahold of them directly via phone or email and ask, "Have you ever heard of retargeting? It's like a boomerang. You basically track website visitors who have never contacted you back to Facebook, where you run a simple offer. You can easily double or triple your conversion rates. Would you like to have a free trial for two weeks so I can show you how to do this?"

Now, what's the marketing manager going to say? She's going to say, "Wow, *free*? What's the catch?"

"All you've got to do is agree to pay a couple of hundred dollars for the ads. Then I'll prove you can find people who visited your website but never bought from you, and we'll get them into your practice."

Notice how you're working your way down from two or three months of complimentary services to just two weeks. If you've followed the previous strategies to this point, then you've got the confidence and the results to start charging for your services.

So here's how you finish the Pixel Helper Strategy—you produce results for the dentist using the Audience Strategy, Messaging Strategy, and Funnel Strategy. At the end of the two-week trial when you've gotten the dentist thirty or forty leads, you'll follow up with the marketing manager, "I'm prepared to give you exclusivity for New York. If you sign a retainer with me, you will be the only dentist in the entire city I work with. My services start at $1,500 per month."

Most clients are going to sign up for the $1,500 retainer to start with, but as time (and new customers) go by, you'll easily justify higher rates. When you approach dentists in other cities—Los Angeles, Seattle, Quebec, London—you'll offer the exact same exclusivity rights. Since you've proven your methods work, they'll be terrified to imagine you giving *their* results to the competition!

Congratulations, you've got your very first paying client for *free*. Now let's go wild with my **fourth strategy**. It's time to build your very first **Funnel** for *your* business. As you recall, the Funnel Strategy starts with the end in mind—that is, your offer. And your offer is going to be a complimentary lead generation audit (your Pixel Helper plus Traffic Analysis), which you'll value at $995.

Let's say you love yoga, so you want to serve the yoga studios niche. Your landing page offer, therefore, will feature simple text like, "Grow your yoga studio. Apply now for your free yoga studio lead generation audit."

Yoga studio owners click the button below your headline, fill out an application form on the next page, and book a session with you in your calendar. (See EliteInc.com/AgencyBookResources for my top scheduling software recommendations.)

In your session, follow the first two steps of the Pixel Helper Strategy—Tracking Pixel, traffic analysis, retargeting explanation. At the end of your conversation, you'll once again offer a free two-week trial to test your methods.

Free is so easy. Everybody loves free. But as soon as you produce results, you'll convert between fifty and seventy-five percent, and sometimes as high as *one hundred* percent of all trial customers into paying retainers. And you'll charge them anywhere from $1,500 to $3,500 per month, depending on how many Avatars they have and Funnels they need. (See Chapter 9 for more on pricing your services).

Once you've got your landing page published, where do you get your next clients from? How do you get more people into your funnel?

My **fifth strategy**, **Database Lists**. All across the world, market research companies sell leads database lists for pennies on the dollar per lead. For example, Agency FastTrack student Curtis bought a list of 18,000 photographers for $100! You can buy a list of plastic surgeons, music store owners, pet salons, or whatever niche you're after. If you know what you want, you can buy it online. (See EliteInc.com/AgencyBookResources for my recommended database list companies.)

So, what do you do with this list? Be *everywhere*. Send a message to their emails. Shoot an SMS text to their mobile phone numbers. And—I kid you not—send out a free digital fax broadcast.

"Niel, dude! I'm supposed to be providing *digital* marketing services. Are you nuts? Why on earth would I go and send a fax to people?"

Now that I've read your mind, let me ask *you* a couple of questions:

How many faxes have you received in the last month? Maybe two or three, if any?

And how many of those faxes did you open? I bet you opened every single one.

Why? Because nobody sends you faxes anymore.

If someone receives your email, and they've got no idea who you are, they may not respond. If they also get an SMS they may think, *Okay, it's the same crowd.* But if they then see a fax from you, they're going to think, *Geez, what a coincidence. I've been seeing these guys all around. Maybe they're worth looking into for generating leads in my niche.* Because you are! You're omnipresent, like some sort of marketing god! The more you market to the same people using different platforms, the more successful you're going to be. They're going to think you're the biggest show in town.

The **sixth strategy** is my simplest yet—**Google Pay Per Click Ads**. If you want to add that New York dentist to your clientele, write headlines like, "Dental Digital Marketing," or, "Free Dentist Website Audit." Very simple, but very effective. Since you're converting at least fifty percent of anyone who accepts your free audit offer into clients, Google PPC ads are your very own online slot machine—ad budget in, clients out!

Google PPC ads are hard to beat, but you can with my **seventh strategy**. **Gmail Ads** allows you to reach the one billion-plus people across the globe who use Gmail; and most of them log into their Gmail accounts *several* times a day.

Before you run that first Gmail Ad, you're going to upload your leads database list for a "Customer Match," to find a percentage of those people on Gmail. In my experience, Google finds about seventy-five percent of people on a leads list on Gmail.

You're going to run ads only to these people with a very simple headline like, "Dentists take note, a new marketing strategy just revealed," or, "Dentists, is your website turning patients away?"

Again, call out to your niche in the ad headline. And like Google PPC, you only pay for the ad when someone clicks it. Gmail Ads are much, much, much cheaper. You can get a click in Gmail Ads for about $0.10 per click, whereas the same click on Google PPC will cost you between $3 and $5. If they *do* click on your ad and read the proposition, chances are they're going to take you up on it and become a client.

For my **eighth strategy**, head on over to **LinkedIn**. Upload your entire database list into Gmail Contacts, then import that list into LinkedIn. Out of Curtis' list of 18,000 people, he found almost 4,700 of them on LinkedIn.

Curtis wrote a custom message with each LinkedIn request, which reads, "Photographers, we provide specialized services to generate leads for photographers. We've got space for two free trial accounts. Click on this link." Every click he gets is *free*.

Just like his Funnel's landing page, which offers a free audit to photographers, Curtis' LinkedIn profile speaks directly to his niche.

Stay on LinkedIn for the **ninth strategy**, the **Sponsored Message**. Similar to Gmail Ads, LinkedIn boasts an advertising path right into people's inboxes. Again, Curtis uploads his database list, writes a message promoting his audit offer, and fires away. Sponsored Messages are the cheapest way to advertise in LinkedIn, but for some weird reason, it's just not common practice, so you've got very little competition.

The **tenth strategy** needs little explanation—**Facebook Ads**. Run them to your niche. Drive traffic to your free audit landing page. Watch leads fill up your inbox.

The **eleventh strategy** takes us back to your inbox. A **Solo Mailer** is a one-time sponsored email message to highly qualified potential clients. Let's say your niche is the hunting industry, and you want to promote your services to professional hunters.

Where do they hang out? What societies or associations do they belong to? You're going to pay a visit to those professional hunter organizations' websites and see which offer promotional opportunities to advertisers like you. You'll pay the organization a one-time fee, give them your ad with your marketing message and call-to-action, and they'll blast your email to the entire membership list. Instantly, you reach a few thousand (or more) potential clients overnight.

Display Ads are the **twelfth strategy**, and they're very similar to the Solo Mailer. A lot of niche websites like the professional hunter associations allow advertisers to rent advertising space in the header, right hand side, and inline text of their website. Whether it's an association website, trade show website, or niche publication, their ad costs are usually very, very cheap.

Unlike the previous few strategies, my **thirteenth strategy** is completely free. List your advertising services on **Freelance Portals** like Fiverr, Upwork, and Freelancer. You don't pay for a listing; if small business owners find you on any of these platforms and book you, you pay the site a very small (and fair) fee. Even though these platforms are quite crowded, I find Agency FastTrack students get overwhelmed with the massive amount of people looking for highly qualified digital marketing specialists. Like your LinkedIn profile, make your Freelance Portals' profile niche-specific. Serve kitchen cabinet manufacturers? Put them in your profile name, and you'll show up as the top result whenever potential clients search "digital marketing for kitchen cabinet manufacturers!"

With my **fourteenth strategy**, you're getting the word out about your agency using **Free Directory Services**. In South Africa, we have a service called Gumtree, the equivalent to Craigslist in the United States. Yes, posting an ad for your business seems elementary, but you won't believe how many people use the platform to look for service providers. They won't find you if you're not there! So post your free lead generation audit, and watch as appointments fill your schedule.

Lastly, my **fifteenth strategy** requires the least amount of effort—**Appointment Making Services**. These third party lead generating companies charge you for appointments they book with potential clients they find for you, not for hours worked. What an incredible deal!

Choose an Appointment Maker, and give them the leads database list you've been messaging via email, SMS, and fax as well as a very simple script along the lines of, "Hello, I'm following up on the messages you've been getting from us about your free marketing audit. Would you like to sign up for that today?" (See EliteInc.com/Agency-BookResources for my service provider recommendations.)

By this point, you've probably had to walk away from the book just to wrap your head around the first few strategies. Which strategies will work the best for you? And where should you start?

I'll tell you what I always tell Agency FastTrack students—**start at the beginning**! Start with Practice Clients, work your way up to Free Trial clients, and then book your very first Retainer clients. You may have your VA create a system for four or five strategies, a new one each month, and a few months from now, you're earning upwards of $10,000 per month.

In fact, it's *impossible* to not succeed if you and your VA stick with these system-driven strategies. Let's say you want to reach that magic $10,000 per month within the next ten months. If you're not super confident yet, maybe you won't start at $1,500 retainers, you start at $1,000 per month. That means you need ten total clients, one new client per month.

If you are the world's worst salesperson, you'll close maybe ten percent of strategy calls (more on strategy calls in Chapter 9). Do the math, and you and your VA have a measurable goal—one hundred strategy calls total, ten strategy calls per month, two or three strategy calls per week. Boom! You've got yourself a six-figure digital agency in less than a year.

And if you follow any one of these strategies properly, you may never need all of them! Once your Virtual Assistant has got you at capacity, ask them to pause your marketing until you're ready to expand the agency. In fact, I hope you *do* get so overwhelmed with business that you don't have to market for long. That means you get to be picky with your clients. A very, very good thing. As long as you have a careful vetting process, you won't have to work with those clients that drain your time and sap your energy! Let me show you how I vet.

CHAPTER 8

BUCK OR MOUSE? VETTING YOUR CLIENTS

The average lion eats roughly twenty-five pounds of meat per day. To satisfy his appetite, a lion has a couple of options: he either chases small rodents, or bigger game. Field mice are normally rampant, so the lion might hunt what's easiest to chase, kill, and chew. But mice are a couple of ounces each. Time chasing field mice adds up. Just to keep from starving, the lion would have to eat over two hundred mice per day! Higher up in the food chain (and in protein content!) sits the buck, weighing in at three hundred pounds. Do the math! Just one of these guys nets the lion nearly two weeks' worth of meals.

A couple of hundred hunts per day, or just one hunt every other week. If you were the lion, which would you choose? Hold your answer for a second. Because *most* digital agency owners stalk mice, not buck. And when they do spot a big, juicy buck, they scurry into the weeds and hide.

As an agency, you're going to find a lot of mice. They're too small for you. They can't pay you. And they make up about ninety-five percent of your prospects! Say no to the field mice. Newbies think they can take on small clients and help them succeed, but that's a lot of rubbish. Keep your eye on the buck. Just because there are more field mice doesn't mean you should chase them. You'll feel spent after a day's worth of hunting only to find yourself hungrier than when you started.

Just as you had a marketing system involving a VA, a dashboard, and strategies you methodically test, you've got to have a **vetting strategy** for all the leads pouring into your inbox. Most will be field mice, a few will be bucks. Unless you know what to look for in a client, you might go chasing what looks like a herd of buck, only to find mice leading you off the buck's scent.

When I ask Agency FastTrack students what differences they've spotted between their buck leads and mouse leads, I've gotten ten consistent answers.

"Good quality clients can afford my services."

"They're already successful businesses, not failing ones."

"They're eager to invest in their business, and they have funds set aside to do so."

"They're organized and on time."

"They're fairly easy going, not control freaks."

"Their industry will be in demand for years to come."

"Their products are easy to sell, plain and simple."

So, how do you turn this information into a practical vetting strategy to use on your prospects?

Here's how you'll distinguish bucks from mice. Let's say you're on a strategy call with a prospect. She's telling you all about her business model, what her customers love about her products, and what she's looking for from an agency like yours. You've got a good feeling about her, but you're not sure. Is she a buck, or is she a mouse?

Buck clients can afford your services, mouse clients can't. If her business cannot afford a $1,500 per month retainer, she's not the business for you, period. Since most SMBs in North America budget five hundred bucks a month for marketing, most leads you get contacting you will be field mice. No matter how tempting, don't work with them.

That means you've got to believe that there ARE people willing to pay $1,500 per month, and there are! If two or three leads balk at your pricing, you might feel what's called "Imposter Syndrome."

Am I really credible? Do I really know what I'm doing? Should I really charge this much?

CHAPTER 8 - BUCK OR MOUSE? VETTING YOUR CLIENTS

Who exactly are you comparing yourself to? It's easy to imagine a group of agency owners with superior skills who call you out as a fraud online. Trust me, that won't happen!

Compare yourself to your average client. How much do they know about Avatars, Funnels, and Tracking Pixels? Chances are, not much! Look up the big brands you use every day. How many of them grasp something as simple as a Tracking Pixel? Many businesses, especially the ones with your target $1,500 per month budget, want to capitalize on the digital marketing opportunity, but they don't have the time or talent to do so.

That's why they need you. But if you've got no time for them, thanks to a handful of field mice clients who pay you $500 per month or less, they'll go find somebody else.

Buck clients would succeed without you, mouse clients won't succeed at all.

So, back to your strategy call. Ask about her track record. Has she dominated her industry? Is the competition chasing her? Is she the biggest, fastest, or best priced?

If so, she's probably a buck. She does not need you to succeed because she already has! So, why would she hire you? Because you're going to help her *succeed faster and better* than she would without you.

Bucks are a joy to work with. They show up on time, know what they're doing, and trust your expertise. Mouse clients, on the other hand, barely pay their bills. They have a sour attitude. They trash talk competitors.

Pity them, yes, but don't let them hire you! They won't show up on time, they won't know how to follow up with the leads you provide, and they'll doubt you at every turn.

Buck clients think like investors, mouse clients think like employees.

Bucks see marketing as an investment. In fact, you'll hear them talking about the campaigns they're already running, maybe print ads in local newspapers or radio ads. They're talking to you about digital marketing because you know how to provide them with a better ROI than these traditional methods have.

But field mice clients take their self-employment a little too seriously. They're just that—*employed*. And employees don't spend money on their businesses. Ever. Just the *idea* of parting with a hundred bucks makes them sweat. If you do get lucky enough to convince a mouse to invest in marketing, they'll quit if their first $100 doesn't net them a thousand inquiries. You're wasting your time.

Buck clients are organized, mouse clients are a mess.

If you work with a structured, disciplined business, they'll be able to measure the ROI your services offer and justify your retainer for years to come. In fact, you should expect every buck to stay with you for five to seven years, meaning your *least* profitable client is worth $90,000 over time!

You'll be lucky if mice ever pay you on time. Their businesses exist in a perpetual state of chaos where the owner acts as the accountant, customer service specialist, and janitor...all over the course of an hour! They can't track their ROI on your services, much less whether or not they paid you!

Buck clients are easygoing, mouse clients are obnoxious.

When you're talking to a buck on your strategy call, you won't feel like you're selling her. You'll feel the chemistry between you. She's happy to invest in your high ROI services because it's clear you know your stuff. She might ask to have a look at two or three references before signing an agreement, but that's as difficult as she gets.

Mice are just obnoxious. They treat you like you're a replaceable service provider. They might even say so to your face! You're anxious about every upcoming call with mice because they overlook what matters. They'll lose the Avatar worksheet you completed together, all the while spending thirty minutes telling you what color to make that one tiny button at the bottom of their landing page. Don't be surprised if you fire them before they fire you!

Buck clients have industry longevity, mouse clients don't.

Before you hop on a call with a prospect, do your homework. Is the business established in a growing industry that'll be around five to seven years from now? Or is their entire industry nearing sunset?

CHAPTER 8 - BUCK OR MOUSE? VETTING YOUR CLIENTS

Most staffing businesses, for example, are bucks. As more and more corporations transition from full-time staff to temp-to-hire workers, staffing businesses barely keep up with demand. Half a decade from now, I bet staffing will be a top ten industry in most industrialized countries.

Mice are the opposite. Their industries are disappearing, fading into irrelevance or serving up as a snack for bigger businesses. If you're talking to an independent clothing retailer whose competitors all got bought up by big box brands, no Funnel can save them from the inevitable.

Buck clients require a short selling cycle, mouse clients need a much longer cycle.

Landing Page, Free Offer, First Appointment—if that's how easy it is to close the sale, they're a buck. Think dentists with the free teeth cleaning appointments.

Be wary of a business, no matter how successful, which takes weeks or longer to close a single sale. For example, it's not unheard of for IT consultants to pass proposals back and forth for five or six months with their customers before the sale happens. IT consultants are big mice, yes, but not mice you want on your plate.

Buck clients' products are an easy sell, mouse clients' aren't.

"Commodity" is a dirty word in digital marketing, but to your $1,500 per month retainer business, it's pure as the white snow capping Mount Everest. Commodity products and services are a remarkably easy sell. Think office furniture or veterinarians, both uncomplicated businesses. As long as offices and pets exist, demand for new office furniture and vets exists, too. The fewer interactions a prospective customer has to have with a business before they're sold on the product, the more likely the business is a buck.

Careful not to let mice lure you in with their trendy, one-of-a-kind products or services. If you're talking to a life coach, you're talking to a mouse. If you're talking to a digital training program creator, you're talking to another mouse. Let them hire your competitors instead—they'll spin their wheels for months and get nowhere.

Buck clients have high margin products, mouse clients have low margins.

Remember our plastic jewelry business from Chapter 1? A classic mouse business. At two or three bucks per sale, you'll go mad trying to sell $500 worth of bracelets per month, and you won't even get *close* to giving the business a return on your $1,500 retainer.

You're more likely to find deer among high-end service providers like chiropractors, luxury products like decorative concrete coaters, and medical professionals like dentists.

Buck clients give you repeat business, mouse clients offer a once-off project.

With a buck business, one sale automatically leads to the next. Once you sign up for a dentist's free teeth cleaning, you're happy to get that cavity fixed. Then you schedule your teeth whitening appointment, corrective oral surgery, and so on.

Hire a photographer specializing in graduations for your kid's high school graduation and…that's it. You won't be hiring them again. Such clients look attractive at first, but don't be fooled by the high profit margin. The secret to high ROI services made easy is to send leads to your clients who buy again and again and again. One lead, one customer, multiple sales a year.

To vet your sales calls in real time, download this handy cheat-sheet. All you do is go to EliteInc.com/AgencyBookResources

CHAPTER 8 - BUCK OR MOUSE? VETTING YOUR CLIENTS

BUCK CLIENTS VS MOUSE CLIENTS

Buck Clients	Mouse Clients
Can afford your services	Can't afford your services
Would succeed without you	Won't succeed at all
Think like investors	Think like employees
Are organized	Are a mess
Are easygoing	Are obnoxious
Have industry longevity	Don't have industry longevity
Require a short selling cycle	Need a much longer cycle
Products are an easy sell	Aren't an easy sell
Have high margin products	Have low margins
Give you repeat business	Offer a one-off projects

Elite Inc.

So, the table is now set. You know which clients will sustain your agency and which won't. But unless you know how to close the deal with a buck, you won't be eating any buck steaks tonight.

CHAPTER 9

CLOSE THE DEAL: SALES, PRICING, AND ONBOARDING

I hate job interviews.

You're sitting there powerless, sweat trickling down the back of your shirt. The interviewer studies your resume or CV, reading closely for any reason to disqualify you from the job...and from your future. Every interview question comes across like an accusation.

"What makes you think you're qualified for this position?"

"If I asked your last employer what your top five weaknesses are, what would they tell me?"

"Tell me about a time you failed very, very badly."

You've got the perfect answers in your head...but something completely different falls out of your mouth. The interviewer stares at you and *through* you with a deadpan face.

"Thank you." The interviewer cuts you off mid-sentence. "That will be all."

Job interviews suck.

Fortunately, sales conversations bear ZERO resemblance to them them—IF you know how to sell *properly*. And that's exactly what I'm going to teach you how to do.

By this point in the book, you've got nearly everything you need to talk with your leads one-on-one and convert as many bucks as possible into tasty retainer clients. You've adopted a strategic mindset, and you understand how Audiences, Messaging, and Funnels work together to produce high returns on clients' investment. Meanwhile, you may be picking up the prerequisite digital marketing skill sets through free online tutorials or a fast-paced, results-oriented program like Agency FastTrack. You know how to generate leads for your agency and tell a buck from a mouse.

Nearly **everything you need**.

Actually *turning* a lead into a client is scary stuff if the only sales experience you have is being sold to (at a used car lot, let's say) or doing your best to sell yourself (at a job interview). In Agency FastTrack, I take a very different approach to selling. Remember, your digital agency is a small business' greatest ally, their most valuable asset, their partner on a profitable growth journey. So if you go into a sales call with the mentality you've got to *prove* yourself, you certainly won't. The prospect will cross-examine you like it's a job interview, and they'll leave the conversation doubting your every word.

If you're not on equal footing with your leads (or higher), you're toast. The only way to get there is to get your clients knowing, liking, and trusting you *before* they become clients—before they even get the chance to.

Having your very own Funnel is key for booking a sales call with you, because you won't *call* it a sales call. A Funnel's offer is a low-friction entry point into your business, remember? What you're going to do is replace the idea of a sales call with a *free strategy call* where your leads receive a free digital marketing audit. I'll unpack all of this in a moment, but first, how do you get people to book this free strategy call in the first place?

No matter which lead generation strategy you and your Virtual Assistant start with, you're going to drive everyone to the same place—your free strategy call offer landing page. Of course, not everyone is going to sign up on the spot. So you're going to *retarget* every visitor to your landing page, just as you will with your clients who get traffic on their websites. On both Facebook and Google, you're going to run retargeting ads to *only* those people who've visited your landing page. (You have a Tracking Pixel on your landing page, so this is a breeze!)

However, the *last* thing you want is to show up on a video call with R.E.A.D.Y. stage one or stage two prospects. These leads aren't really leads. They don't know, like, or even trust digital marketing as the best solution for their business' growth needs, much less know, like, or trust you. So your retargeting ads are going to "warm them up," moving them from early buying stages of awareness to red-hot interest levels. To do this, you'll need to run two types of retargeting ads:
1. Good quality blog articles
2. Client testimonial videos

Notice, you're not sending people right back to the landing page. You're building up some credibility in their minds *first*. Then, both the articles and the videos feature a link to the free strategy call landing page.

While testimonial videos are fairly easy to produce—just record a past client talking for thirty to sixty seconds about how you helped grow their business—articles can be tricky. I see way too many digital agency owners publish blogs that give away the family farm, so to speak. They write these five thousand-word epics, detailing every single strategy and tactic they use to generate leads. With content like that, what the hell does a business need you for?

Instead, you're going to answer small business owners' questions related to hiring an agency. Write and publish ten or twelve total two thousand-words tops articles answering questions *already* floating around in your prospective clients' heads, including:

- "What's a 'Funnel,' and how is it different from my website?"
- "How do I know if digital marketing will work for *my* business?"
- "How expensive is digital marketing?"
- "Which online platform is best to generate leads?"
- "What are the differences between Facebook, Google, and LinkedIn advertising?"
- "What should my company's digital marketing budget be?"
- "What should I pay per lead or per client when running an advertising campaign?"

Refer back to Messaging Strategy in Chapter 5 for my best tips on writing blog articles. If you're time-strapped, ask your VA to write the first drafts of each article for you to touch up and publish. To make this task even easier, use those questions as the *titles* of your blog articles and just type out your best answer!

After reading two or three of these articles, most of the prospects who left your landing page without signing up will change their minds. But because you don't know *which* articles will do the trick, put five bucks a day behind each of the articles in your retargeting campaign, and run the ads for thirty days or until you've booked so many strategy calls you're having to cut back on sleep and skip meals!

An added benefit of retargeting is who *else* sees them—leads who actually DID book a strategy call! In the day or two between their booking and the scheduled call, they'll see your blog articles and testimonial videos showing up in their news feeds and internet searches, proving you're capable, building your credibility, and increasing the likelihood they'll show up on the call ready to part with money.

Now, you can skip all of this if you like and instead devote your free time to mastering your sales skills. But in my experience, ninety-nine percent of people resist the hard sell. And even most salespeople aren't brilliant at pushing people to sign up for a long-term retainer contract in twenty or thirty minutes, including me! I'd much rather avoid that nerve-wrecking conversation and be a digital marketing doctor who diagnoses a small business owner's marketing mistakes, website weaknesses, and advertising opportunities.

That means you've got to show up with your facts straight. Take twenty or thirty minutes before your first (or next) strategy call and have a look at your lead's website and social media profiles.

Use one of my recommended traffic analysis tools and resources to see how many visits the site receives per month. Then check to see whether or not they have a Tracking Pixel installed on their website. Make a note of what you find. Next, head over to their social media profiles. How many total followers and fans do they have across all social platforms, from Facebook and Instagram to LinkedIn and Twitter? Do they post often on any of these platforms, or are they digital ghost towns? Include all of your findings in a single-page report to review on your call. Just the fact that you did your homework on their business will blow their minds.

That simple report—often called an "audit"—is the starting point for the strategy call. Not you, your agency, or your experience. Frame the conversation around *their* business, not yours, and you're off to the best possible start. That way, you'll be able to explain *exactly* how you will generate a return on their advertising investment. For example, even if they're not ready to sign a retainer agreement, at the very least they'll be excited to sign up for a short-term trial campaign.

The trial offer is going to be your best friend when you're just starting out. It's based on what my marketing mentor Jay Abraham calls, "Risk Reversal."[1] The idea is, you're taking all the risk of the campaign not working *off* of your client's budget. They're only committing to one or two months to start, and they can leave at that time if they're not happy.

Remember the dating metaphor? If marketing is like dating, then your strategy call is equivalent to the first couple of dates. You're getting to know each other, you're building rapport, and you're kicking off a relationship. So the short-term trial offer is like asking the other person to be your boyfriend or girlfriend. It's not this huge, unexpected marriage proposal coming out of nowhere. Retainers aren't worth the paper they're written on if there's no trust. People marry because their relationship has *proven* mutually beneficial. If it doesn't work for either person, it's over. Your retainer is similar. If you tell a client you'll do a sixty-day trial to test out the relationship and achieve one specific objective, their risk is limited, and both parties get to test out the relationship. Yes, there *will* be people who are in R.E.A.D.Y. stage five, meaning they're totally sold on your long-term retainer agreement straightaway. But most of your leads, even the bucks, will feel a lot more comfortable with a significantly less risky trial agreement.

On your strategy call, your primary job isn't to "sell" the short-term trial campaign, it's to determine how long it will take to produce ROI. If you want to upsell your client into that long-term retainer, create measurable results. Results speak for themselves, no extra selling necessary.

Let's say you're dealing with a small business that has a huge Facebook following, maybe ten to twenty thousand people, and posts a lot of content. You might only need two or three *weeks* to get this business results. You'd create your Funnel and run Facebook ads *directly* to these followers who already know, like, and trust the business. If they also have a Tracking Pixel installed on their website, create an audience based on previous website traffic and send those people right into a Funnel. Even if the campaign stumbles, your client will get probably twenty new paying customers, which more than justifies further investment.

Basically, you're reaching for that low-hanging fruit first, those people in stage five of the R.E.A.D.Y. model. Target customers who are most likely to buy during your trial period, then open your services up and run ads to the other stages once they rehire you.

With this end in mind, **here's how you *begin* your strategy call**:

"I had a look at a few things on your website and your social media. Let's review what I found…"

Then, tell them what you found! It's a very, very simple way to demonstrate your digital marketing expertise while being helpful. Chances are, no one has ever walked them through their traffic numbers before.

Explain your findings with what *you* can offer in mind. For example, you might say, "I found that you get ten thousand visitors a month. Fantastic! But you don't have a Tracking Pixel installed. You are driving traffic with PPC ads on Google, but you're not retargeting those visitors with Facebook ads and sending them into a Funnel."

"Let's switch back over to you. What are some of your business objectives today?"

Your second question is very, very strategic. Notice, you're *not* asking them what digital marketing they'd like to try. If you did ask, they'd probably tell you what they *think* they should do. But you want the person telling you exactly what business goals they have, separate from anything to do with digital marketing.

They might say, "Well, I want customers, and I want a better way of weeding out people who aren't a good fit for my business."

"Great! You want more customers. What are you battling with to try to achieve your goal?"

Your third question helps you—and them—see where the gap is. You want them taking ownership over their serious problem, which needs an equally serious solution. The more serious they are, the more money they'll feel prepared to put down.

For example, your lead might tell you, "We used to get lots of walk-in traffic, but it's dropped. I'm really worried about the long-term health of the business. Revenue from my regulars has been consistent, but we need to try something different to get new customers."

Then, it's your job to label the problem. Let them take ownership in their own words. "So, your problem is not enough feet through the door?" you'd ask.

"Yes, that's my problem."

From there, discover any biases they might have against the digital agency solution.

"Have you tried digital marketing in the past to solve your problem?"

On the journey toward the sale, your real enemy is negative preconception. Your lead may believe Facebook is falling apart after the Cambridge Analytica scandal. Someone might have told them Google ads don't work.

If your lead tells you, "Yes, we tried it, but it didn't work," they're *really* asking you to explain *why* it failed. Without an explanation, they have no reason to give digital marketing another go.

"I Boosted a few posts on Facebook. Nothing happened," your lead says.

You reply with a few follow up questions. "In those posts, did you target a specific audience? Did you ask people to take a specific action?"

"Well...no. I guess I didn't."

And the light bulb goes off! What you're doing with these questions is proving that the platform itself isn't to blame, it's the way they *used* the platform. As a result, they come to the conclusion they need your help...but without you having to say so.

Then bring the conversation back to their specific goals.

"Okay, cool. So again, you want more feet in your store. Can you quantify that? What are your measures of success? And how far are you from where you want to be?"

This question gets into what's called a "Gap Analysis," which is determining how wide the gap is between a business' goals and their present state and what it'll take to close the gap.

If you're talking to someone who owns a hairdressing salon, you could add in a question about the salon's capacity, like, "How many more haircuts can your employees do per day?"

"Both of my hairdressers are at half capacity right now. They could probably do five more per day," she might reply.

"Okay, so you want five more haircuts per day, which is one hundred over the next month. That's what success looks like?"

"Yes! How do you plan to do that?"

If you do *any* selling at all, it's with your very next set of questions.

"Based on what I see, we'll get you leads off Facebook and Google over a two-month trial period. We want to answer a couple of questions during our trial period: 'Can we achieve your goal in a manner that's financially palatable to you, and does our relationship work for both of us?'"

Probably nine times out of ten, your lead will immediately say, "Okay, great. How much does it cost?"

Any question related to price is a buying signal—they're nearly ready!

"It's $1,500 per month for my agency's services plus $500 in ad spending, but there's no contract at this point, just a short-term commitment," you'll say. Then comes the close. "If we're successful and we like working together two months from now, we'll talk about what it looks like to move forward with a retainer agreement. Are you ready to get started?"

At this point, they have only two options: yes or no. If it's yes, their demeanor will change. They'll look bright, chipper, and hopeful. "Send over the paperwork. I'm ready to get started."

However, if their answer is no, they won't actually *say* no. They might say something like, "Let me think it over. Can you send a proposal?"

Do not send the proposal. Repeat: **DO NOT SEND THE PROPOSAL**.

"No," easily becomes "Yes," if you address the prospect's silent objections and provide a satisfactory answer. So you'll reply to the proposal request with something like, "The proposal puts in writing what we've discussed today. Is there anything specific you want to know about that we haven't covered?"

At that point, they'll whip out the most common objections to digital marketing, including, "How do I know it will work for me?" or, "How soon will I make my investment back?"

Of course, you've already written articles answering these questions! So all you have to do is pull up the objection-specific blog article on your computer and read off the highlights, effectively countering the objection. Then wrap the chat back around to your close.

"With that in mind, shall we do a trial and see how it goes?"

You may have to cycle from objection to answer, objection to answer a few times. But if you've got a buck on that call, expect a final answer like, "Yes. Send over the paperwork, and we'll get started. How do I pay you?"

Because there's still a slim chance they'll blow you off, commit to sending over the documentation along with an invoice and ask for commitment in return.

"When is the best time in your schedule this week to kick off the trial? We're going to complete a couple of worksheets together to ensure you're off to a good start."

You don't have to explain the Avatar workshop in detail. In fact, it's better not to throw too much information at them when the prospect's in a buying mood.

From there, use a proposal software to send your new client an agreement they can e-sign to make your two-month trial official. *Never send over traditional paperwork*. Business owners hate printing, reading, signing, scanning, and sending back proposals. For both agreements and invoices, use an automation solution. Check out my latest recommendations at EliteInc.com/AgencyBookResources.

Ideally, at the start of your relationship, you both know exactly what KPI's you're aiming for: new leads, new customers, new revenue. Maybe the client has other objectives like brand exposure or more engagement with an existing customer base. Whatever success looks like, make sure the objective is written clearly in your agreement so you're both (literally) on the same page.

In your agreement, you'll also cover the agreed-on budget—both your retainer services and their advertising budget they'll reimburse you for. Include a quick sentence about timelines as well. For example, when are you scheduling your worksheet meetings? When can they expect the Funnel to be ready? What is the projected trial kickoff?

To make sure you have the best chances of success possible, make the creative sign-off process clear. Write into your agreement when you expect your client to approve copy, images, ads, and whatever else that needs to run. Take leadership in the relationship—as long as you don't run over-budget, your client will not be able to interfere in a campaign they've already approved.

Get agreement on the scope of work to avoid "scope creep," which is when the client asks for a new logo, new website copy, and a new Funnel. You're willing to take on more work, but make very, very clear in your agreement what your trial offer includes and does not include. If you're producing, you're getting paid—it's that simple.

Minimize your communication as well. If you want a six-figure agency, you can't field two or three calls from the same client every day. Set expectations in your agreement.

And most importantly, you've got to cover their leads tracking and reporting. What software will your client use to track every call, every inquiry, every message? If they have a CRM already they can provide access to, you're good to go. Every single week, provide a leads report and debrief your client on what's working and what's not. You'll be seen as an absolute pro through these conversations.

Now, the CRM brings up another issue unrelated to the trial agreement. How do you get access to what you need? Despite everyone's best intentions, it can sometimes be excruciating to get the information from your clients you need to start the process.

Provide a low-friction way of getting what you need. Send your client a laundry list of to-do's, and they'll leave it in the inbox without responding. You're better off asking for one or two things at a time.

If they don't know where to find something—their company logo, for example—just ask them for their graphic designer's contact information. That way, you can get what you need *and* build relationships with their team members.

I also recommend providing structure to your relationship. Free online project management software keeps both of your responsibilities top of mind, and they'll know *why* you need what you need. For example, you could include a quick checklist of files you need from them before you can design their Funnel's landing page.

Once you've written all of these things into your agreement, the agreement is signed, the first invoice is paid, and expectations are set, the last thing you need is accountability. Yes, it's intangible, but you need accountability to maintain balance in your relationship. You don't want to succumb to scope creep or lose composure. Be patient with your clients. Always refer back to the agreement if you're battling over a question. If they're late on delivering something to you, let them know they're late. And no matter what, never compromise on fairness. Every successful relationship is about balance, equity, and win-win.

Congratulations! You're starting your new business-agency partnership off right. Produce consistent results, and you've got yourself revenue secured for at least the next five to seven years. As you onboard three, five, even ten new clients and perfect your internet advertising process, you'll want to venture into cross-sell and upsell opportunities. After all, your competition is building websites, applications, and more while stuck in the feast or famine income cycle. But *you've* started at the right place. From where *you* start, your possibilities are endless. Let me show you the happy ending that never ends.

CHAPTER 10

SCALING FOR THE FUTURE: THE SECRET TO EXPLODE YOUR AGENCY'S PROFITS

"**C**an you help?" These are the most profitable words you'll ever hear a client utter. As you generate leads for small businesses and help them acquire customers via the internet, something very, very strange happens: they no longer judge you on the basis of ROI alone. Of course they expect your campaigns to produce a return, there's no question about that. I'm referring to all the other needs your clients have which aren't as easily measured as lead generation.

As you transition from your trial offer to a retainer relationship, you'll learn more and more about your clients' needs. And because they now trust you with their lead generation, they're open to other ways you can help.

"I want to redevelop my website. Can you help?"

"We need a business app our customers can download. Can you help?"

"It's time to rebrand. That means new logos, graphics, everything. Can you help?"

Whenever you hear questions like these (and you will, because your services are proving profitable), it's the tip-off that you've become the go-to services provider for all things digital. That's the thing about entrepreneurs—they want shortcuts. They want to streamline everything. They don't want two or three different freelancers or contractors, just one strategic growth partner they can trust with everything.

That's you.

With these other projects they'll ask you about, they won't expect an immediate return. Just because a new logo doesn't turn around and produce ten new leads a day doesn't mean your client won't want one.

You don't even have to wait for your clients to ask you for extra help. You can be proactive and add a brief section to your weekly Funnel performance reports mentioning the other services available to them to grow their digital presence. Even if just two or three clients say yes, your revenue goes up dramatically.

Of course, that introduces a slight problem—you're a lead generation and customer acquisition specialist, not a website developer or graphic designer. So how could you, in good conscience, answer, "Yes!" when a client asks, "Can you help?"

Before the internet, advertising agencies grew by hiring full-time employees who worked in a corporate office surrounded by foosball tables. Nowadays, with virtual skills so accessible to anyone with an internet connection, you can acquire a global workforce to help you (and your clients) on-demand.

In the first months of your agency, you're doing everything yourself—strategy calls, client onboarding, campaign setup. You'll run short on time. The best way to keep up with your schedule *and* meet your clients' very profitable needs is to acquire one more skill: **project management.**

Just because your New York City dentist client gives you their website redesign project doesn't mean you should do it yourself. All you need to do is become good at finding and managing third-party service providers with SEO and WordPress knowledge. Find the right service providers, and you can get an incredible markup, from one to two hundred percent or higher!

Now, I'll be frank. Finding professionals skilled in other disciplines is not easy, but it's doable. I do not suggest you Google around for freelance web designers, pick the cheapest on page one search results, and email them the dentist's website dashboard login credentials. I've actually seen newbie agency owners do exactly this—trust me, it doesn't end well!

As a project manager, you want to retain as much control over your client's project as possible. That means you will NOT advertise to the world that you run a full-service agency. Let your competitors get stuck in the feast or famine cycle of one-off website, design, and app projects. Any additional services you offer are for trusted clients, period. Only if your clients ask you, or if you think they can benefit, will you offer a website makeover, logo redesign, etc.

That said, I'm going to share with you the project management process Agency FastTrack students use to build virtual teams, multiply their revenue, and become the go-to digital services provider for their clients, all while cutting back the hours spent in front of a screen.

The first step in the process might surprise you—**mitigate your fears**. It's totally reasonable to worry that you'll hire a subcontractor off the internet who does a crap job on your client's new website design. The site looks like it was built in 1997, the contact form doesn't work, and the pictures won't load. Your client loses his temper and fires you. Great.

This scenario *can* happen, but it doesn't have to. First of all, you are not hiring for one-off projects. You want to onboard a reliable *team* you can delegate every single client project, from websites and logos to applications and public relations campaigns. Furthermore, just as you let small businesses test drive your services before signing a retainer agreement, you'll hire two or three freelancers to work on *your* website or logo to see who delivers the best result—and just as importantly, who is easiest to work with.

Now, the mechanics of actually *finding* these quality service providers involve a number of different freelancer and contractor hiring platforms. In my experience, Upwork and Fiverr are the best platforms to use, but check out EliteInc.com/AgencyBookResources for my latest recommendations.

Both Upwork and Fiverr allow you to search for a specific service provider such as website designer, app developer, or graphics specialist, then *filter* your results. Filtering alone mitigates at least ninety-nine percent of the risk you face when delegating client projects.

On Upwork, I recommend filtering your search results to *only* include freelancers and contractors whose profiles feature:

→ a 90% minimum job success rating
→ $10,000 plus in billings
→ 1,000 plus hours worked

These criteria alone will reveal the *crème de la crème* in any discipline. Among your search results will be ONLY freelancers with excellent reviews and years of experience. If you go by positive reviews alone, you might hire someone whose friends gave them feedback, not real businesses. The last hire you ever want to make is someone who prefers gaming the system over putting in a good day's work. So when you do find someone who meets the criteria, reach out and offer up a small project ASAP.

In fact, it's not uncommon to find super successful freelancers all around the world who've earned in excess of $300,000 and worked more than five thousand hours. An India-based web design agency I once hired for a project has a ninety-nine percent job success rating, 3,300 jobs completed, 539,000 hours worked, and over seven *million dollars* earned. The chances of this crowd failing your project are slim to none. Yes, if you outsource the nuts and bolts of a project to freelancers in a different country, there might be an initial language barrier to breach and a learning curve for you to get to know each other. That's why you're hiring these freelancers to do *your* website and logo first, after all! But when you're hiring an experienced freelancer with a public profile, positive reviews are as good as gold. All it takes to sink their careers is a scathing review. They'll bend over backwards for you—and your client—to ensure everyone is happy.

When your client wants a non-technical project completed, like a slew of new blog articles or fresh website copy, I do recommend hiring someone who shares your client's native language. For example, if I

CHAPTER 10 - SCALING FOR THE FUTURE: THE SECRET TO EXPLODE YOUR AGENCY'S PROFITS

have another dentist client in London, I'll have a look on Upwork for a United Kingdom-based copywriter rather than someone in the Philippines, eastern Europe, or even South Africa.

All of this advice applies to my second preferred platform, Fiverr. Typically, you'll find freelancers who prefer the one-off jobs looking for work on Fiverr, but you'll still find plenty of quality people. In fact, vetting good quality service providers is even easier than on Upwork, as all you have to do is filter search results for "Top Rated Sellers." To earn this exclusive title, freelancers have to:

- → Use the platform for at least 6 months
- → Complete 100 individual orders
- → Earn at least $20,000
- → Keep a 4.8 out of 5 star rating
- → Respond to at least 90 percent of all inquiries
- → Complete at least 90 percent of all projects
- → Complete at least 90 percent of all projects on time
- → Receive no warnings for spam or inappropriate behavior

It should go without saying—any freelancer with a Top Seller Rating is indeed a top professional.

Risk mitigation really is this simple. Leverage the authentic reputation and real-life experience of freelancers from all around the world to build your team, and you can easily double or triple the annual revenue of every client you already have.

That said, hiring a remote team you trust is only one aspect of project management. There is, of course, the project itself! Even when you hire the highest rated freelancer to help with a project, there's still a risk that they complete the job on time, but the deliverable turns out nothing like what the client expected. To mitigate this risk and manage every project well, you'll want to write very detailed project briefs and get your client's approval before sharing them with your virtual team.

A professional brief includes four detailed sections: **success, timeline, budget,** and **milestones.**

Begin with the end in mind. In the very first paragraph of your single-page document, explain what the end result looks like. How do you, your client, and your contractor all know the job was done well and deserves an excellent review? Keep your definition of **success** to three to five specific things, so as not to overwhelm anyone. Wherever you're tempted to use a nebulous term like "quality," replace the word with a vivid description. What, exactly, does quality look like? If you're asking for a "quality" logo, attach a collection of five to ten company logos to the brief and state what your client likes about each one. This way, you now have a shared definition of "quality," and everyone knows what success looks like.

Next up is the **timeline**. When is your client ready to begin the project, and when must the project *absolutely* be done? Replace your client's deadline with your own to give yourself at least one week's time to review your freelancer's work before submitting to your client. This relieves the pressure in case you and your freelancer need to go back and forth a couple of times to tweak this or that section of your client's new website.

Cover **budget** and **milestones** in the same section of your detailed brief. Separate the project into stages, then assign a budget to each stage. These milestones keep everyone focused on that one part of the project, ensuring it's a success, before moving onto the next. The last thing you want is a deliverable your client doesn't want, and a freelancer who still needs to get paid for it. Milestones and budget constraints prevent this headache altogether.

For example, the first milestone of a website design project is the initial mockup of the site itself. Once the client approves the design and submits payment for the milestone to you, you pay your freelancers their share and move on to the next milestone.

If your freelancer charges you $2,500 for the entire website project, follow my recommendation from earlier in this chapter. Quote your client a one to two hundred percent markup, $5,000 or $7,500. Everyone wins. Your client gets a fantastic, inexpensive website, your freelancer fills their schedule, and you learn just how profitable, "Can you help me?" really is!

CHAPTER 10 - SCALING FOR THE FUTURE: THE SECRET TO EXPLODE YOUR AGENCY'S PROFITS

Job details

Market & Customer Research

Posted 11 months ago

I need someone to help me research all the available targeting options for Facebook Advertising.

We run an automated webinar campaign for our Facebook Ads course and we want to create a hot free download to give to people when they register for our webinar.

In the attached PDF documents you will see two companies who each did a stellar job of listing all the available targeting options.

I want to create a document similar to these two - just better!

Specifically, I want all the latest targeting options available in the US as of today.

I also want a short description of each targeting type so that someone not familiar with Facebook Ads will be able to understand easily.

The document needs to be compiled in such a way that a graphic designer will be able to create a stunning infographic out of it.

$100	$$$ Expert level	December 26, 2017
Fixed-price	I am willing to pay higher rates for the most experienced freelancers	Start Date

Attachments (2)
- Facebook-Targeting-Infographic-WordStream.pdf (1.3 MB)
- advertisemint-complete-guide-facebook-ad-targeting.pdf (2.7 MB)

Project Type: One-time project

Skills and expertise

Facebook Marketing   Internet Research   Market Research

Preferred qualifications

Job Success Score: At least 90%
Include Rising Talent: Yes

Elite Inc.

I highly recommend you add project management to your skill set and meet your clients' expanding needs. As you can see, successful outsourcing and delegation requires a little bit of homework, but once you know exactly what to look for in a freelancer and how to manage your team through a project, you'll be ready to *replace yourself* if you want to. Once you replace yourself, you're set to reach a payday most people can't even imagine. Whether or not you *want* to sell your agency, at least build your business like you will. Because one day, *you may not have a choice.*

CHAPTER 11

BUILT TO SELL: ACHIEVING THE ULTIMATE PAYDAY

As a business coach, I see people spend their whole lives building their business. Many of them enjoy their businesses and earn a wonderful living. But they never think about the fact they may want to sell their business one day and start a new chapter of their life.

They don't think like an entrepreneur. *Real* entrepreneurs think strategically about an exit. But that's not why most people start a business. They don't start them so they can sell them. They start them out of self-expression. It's a labor of love for them. It's about passion. A way of impacting the world. A way of earning.

Only when life circumstances change do people start thinking about selling a business. Sometimes it's a midlife crisis. They think, *Wow, what has my life been about? I think I want to take a sabbatical. I want to write a book. I want to change careers. I want to go on a spiritual quest.*

A divorce or a death in the family can change your perspective in a similar way. *What if I don't wake up tomorrow? I better start pursuing my passion in life. I want to stop doing what I've done all my life.*

For others, a new chapter of life begins. *I want to have a baby, and I don't see this business fitting into that picture.* Or, *It's time to retire and buy that cottage in the Rockies I've always talked about.*

A point will come when you won't want to do this agency thing anymore. The reasons differ, but for most people, that point comes, regardless. And chances are, you can't anticipate what *your* reason will be.

So when your point comes, what are you going to do with everything you've built? If you're like most business owners...*nothing*. Sadly, most people close their businesses. They never realize the value of what they've done. No legacy. No payday. No lump-sum of cash for all their years of effort.

People grossly underestimate what it costs to retire. They don't really have a clue what financial resources will be required to live the life they've subconsciously dreamed of. For you to be able to literally stop working today and be not only financially independent, but financially independent with the lifestyle you want is *much* more expensive than what you think.

The amount of money you need to have invested to pay for your monthly expenses is much bigger than what you imagine. Most people's 401(k)s and retirement savings can fund survival mode, at best. There's definitely no lifestyle to go with it, and I think that's horrible. I think it's an awful idea to work for a lifetime, finally hit retirement one day, and find you have nothing to show for it. What have you got? You've got to live in a small, cheap apartment. You can't travel. You count every cent. If you have unexpected medical expenses, you're forced to dip into your savings. It's awful. I think it's wise to engineer a big payday for yourself, and the sooner you start planning it, the better. At some point, you want to have financial independence.

That's why I tell every new Agency FastTrack student, "Start with the end in mind."

Sure, you may love this digital agency thing once you reach $10,000 a month in recurring revenue. And if you build your business right, you won't be able to imagine doing anything else. But what if the day comes you don't want to do it anymore? What happens to this thing you've built? Can you sell it? Or will you join the ranks of other business owners, surrendering your empire with nothing to show for it?

The time to ask yourself these questions is *not* when that day comes, and it's too late to do anything about it. I know it may not feel very

CHAPTER 11 - BUILT TO SELL: ACHIEVING THE ULTIMATE PAYDAY

real when you're just now starting out. But whether or not you do end up selling your agency, you'll be glad you built your business like you planned to.

The fact is, we entrepreneurs underestimate the energy trade-off we make in our businesses. If I'm a guy in my early thirties bursting with testosterone, I don't mind the crazy hours. I don't mind the red eyes. *I'm going to do this forever, right?*

No, I'm *not* going to do it forever. In a few years, I've got a kid. I won't be sleeping at night. And I'll discover that a family changes everything. I can't put in what I used to put in to my business. So this thing I've built that totally and utterly consumes me, which at the time was cool, is no longer cool.

Always give yourself the option to *not* do what you're doing right now. A good business should be purely optional. If I choose to continue doing it, great. But the day I decide I no longer feel like it, I've got the option not to. The business can work without me.

Build your business like you're going to sell it, and your clients get better service by a mile. Everything happens better and faster. You can build a brand that's not just you—a brand that's actually a business. You're much more likely to be innovative in your work if you've got a business that can work without you. There's space for creativity. There's space for recruiting the right people. You can't do that stuff if you've got your shoulder to the grindstone and you're personally managing every ad campaign yourself.

It's wonderful to have the opportunity to say, "You know, I put seven years into this project. I've done well. I've earned well, and I'm ready to cash out with a big payday." It's incredibly rewarding, both financially and psychologically. It gives you an edge for the next project you want to tackle in life. It makes you a much better entrepreneur if you build a business that will give you an exit one day.

If your paradigm is, "I'm going to just continue hustling and putting out fires to keep the cash and clients flowing," then all you've done is make yourself self-employed. You're not an entrepreneur. You've just created a job. Even if you love it, it's never a good idea to have a business that does not function without you there. There's a time when you either won't *want* to do it anymore—or you won't be *able* to do it anymore.

Case in point—my sister. She had a PhD in Anthropology. One day she asked herself, "Do I love this stuff?" And she said, "No. What do I love?" At the time, she was big into Tantra and meditation. She wanted to become a Tantra teacher.

I said, "You've got a PhD in Anthropology. You know that, right?"

She said, "Yeah, but I'm tired of it."

She became a Tantra teacher, built a following, and taught in thirty-seven different countries across the planet. She was healthy, never smoked anything in her life, didn't drink, and ate an organic and green diet. But when she fell ill suddenly, she couldn't work. She wasn't able to teach her workshops. She couldn't travel, and her business came to a complete standstill.

Sometimes life circumstances prevent you from doing the work you're doing right now. You don't know what's going to happen in your world (or in the world overall), so it's sensible to build a business that can keep working without you. If you can't show up for work for some reason, the business can continue. The only way to really do that right is to focus on building a business you can sell.

Brad Sugars from ActionCOACH defines a business as, "a commercial, profitable enterprise that works without me there."[1] By that definition, most digital agency owners don't have a business. Entrepreneurs have this awful habit of keeping only what they earn on a month-to-month basis in their savings account. It's horrible.

Ask yourself the question, "What do I have to have in place in my business to attract a buyer?" It immediately brings the right governance into your business. You'll start doing things differently—like actually paying yourself a salary. Why? Because you're a damn employee! Separate your earnings from your dividends so you can hire a new CEO to replace you if you ever need to.

If I decide I don't want to do this anymore, I've got absolutely zero problem hiring a CEO—because there's already a salary being paid for a CEO. In that case, I'd just resign, and the day I step out, the new

CEO starts. There's continuity for the business. It's better financial responsibility.

If I don't treat my business like a business, *nobody* will want to buy it. A potential buyer would come and ask, "What dividend is this business going to pay me?"

And I'd tell him, "Oh, don't you worry about it, I've earned a fabulous living. I've lived a great life. Look at me. I've got a big house. I've got two cars. And that's because I'm living off of the business."

The buyer would push back. "Well, that's fantastic, but was this business ever profitable?"

"No, no, I didn't declare profits because I didn't want to pay taxes. So here's how much I earned."

"Rubbish! I'm going to have to *pay* someone what you earned. I'm going to have to hire a high level CEO to run this business, and they're going to earn the same as you. You trying to sell me a business that's not profitable!"

Whether you plan on courting buyers or not, don't make this mistake. The shift from self-employed marketer to digital agency entrepreneur can result in an enormous payday. Agencies sell for a lot of money for a very simple reason—retainer revenue. Very few businesses tie up retainer revenue. You're never going to hear IT companies with service agreements. Built-to-sell agencies are unbelievably attractive because the new owner doesn't need an aggressive marketing and sales team. That's why real estate agencies don't sell for anything. Unless there's hot, well-managed real estate agents in there, it's not making money. Whereas if your digital agency has a hundred clients with systems in place, it sells for a fortune.

Think about it. What does an investor want? As *low* risk and as *high* returns as humanly possible. The very first question a potential buyer is going to ask is, "What's going to happen when the owner is no longer there?"

You're going to show them two assets—your operations and your team. If your business has awesome operating systems that make predictability, reliability, and consistency possible, and a team that stays behind with the business, your buyer is going to be cutting you a very big check.

Let's build operational excellence into your digital agency. Your operations include **systems**, **policies**, and standard operating procedures (**SOPs**). First, let's talk about what each of those things are.

A **system** is anything that happens repeatedly. When you onboard a new client, several things happen every time. You need access to their website. You have to claim their social media pages. You need to create an advertiser account. You have to get the client's company logo and graphics.

If a task like this repeats, you need a system. Sometimes a system is as simple as making a checklist. Other times, it's creating a workflow—if this happens, do *this*; if that happens, do *that*—or a template. If I need to do a client Avatar exercise, I need a client Avatar template.

Policies are do's and don'ts that guide your every business decision. They govern your values. For example, I have a policy in my business that if any task has to be repeated, we create a system. I also have a policy to be on time for meetings. I always say, "Early is on time, and on time is late." In my business, you don't show up late for a meeting. There's no negotiating it. It's a policy that governs behavior.

Another one of my policies is, "No assholes." I absolutely refuse to work with abusive people. Anybody who abuses any of my staff members or causes trouble in a community group gets blocked, deleted, and refunded on the spot.

If systems are *what* you do, **SOPs** are *how* you do them. A procedure is a text-based description of what happens.

Work all of your **systems, policies,** and **standard operating procedures** into your **Digital Agency Operations Manual**. It's a very unsexy document, I know, but an investor won't even look at your business without it. And even if you don't want to sell your agency, you'll still benefit from a manual. You get consistency. Anything that relies on memory in your business won't happen properly. Your manual removes memory from the equation entirely.

Of course, your Operations Manual isn't just for you. As you grow, you'll need to train your employees on "the way we do things around here." And just as any investor wants to see operational excellence, they'll also expect a high performing team.

The very first person you hire is a Virtual Assistant to help market your agency. After that person is in place, you're going to hire your first ad manager. Ad managers are fairly expensive. The current annual median salary for a proficient ad manager in the United States is about $50,000 to $75,000. During the first few months, you teach that person your operations manual.

Why do your ad managers need training? Because very few people have Facebook ad credentials. A lot of people have Google PPC credentials. So you'll probably hire a Google PPC manager with two or three years of experience (or less).

If the campaigns you've built for your clients convert well (and they do, because you followed everything in this book!) you'll want to onboard a freelance Account Manager who specializes in Facebook ad campaigns or Google Ads. This person can reply to comments on your Facebook ads, write your weekly reports, and even handle your strategy calls for you.

Depending on your vision, you can build a multi-person agency with multiple full-time Account Managers and enough consistent revenue to sell your agency to an eager buyer. If you're looking for wealth creation, go for it! The future of your agency all depends on what you're working towards.

At scale, a single ad manager can handle about ten to fifteen clients. Hire your first ad manager once you have about ten clients. At that point, you're going to start drowning a little bit, and your manager will take over one or two of the accounts. As your VA keeps your marketing system running, you'll send your new clients to your ad manager.

Once you have three ad managers who each handle ten to fifteen clients, you can start leveraging their time by adding a person who helps each ad manager generate reports for clients. You can get a low-level, administrative type of person to do that.

You can still keep outsourcing your design for quite a while, but at some point it will start making sense to have a full-time graphic designer.

When you hit the double digit employee mark, start shopping for an operations manager. You're going to feel like you're stretched pretty thin managing all these people, so you want to get a great operations person in place.

From there, you'll want to hire a dedicated salesperson. Your funnels will generate your leads for you, so you need to train someone else to close all those deals in order to move your business to the next level of growth. You want this salesperson dedicated to closing deals.

You're going to have account managers at a ratio of about one to fifteen that will handle your accounts. Typically, your largest employee count is going to be account managers.

If you follow these steps, then over time, you work yourself out of day to day operations, which allows you to accept a leadership role over your team. You start as the person in the trenches. But over time, you move to manager, then entrepreneur. You can't run a digital marketing agency unless you know your digital agency inside and out. You can't get one paying client unless you've got the skills. You figure out how to bring value to your clients. That's your mission. Get that down. *Then* focus on building a business. Hire campaign managers to manage campaigns the way you used to, build funnels the way you used to, onboards new clients the way you used to, and write invoices the way you used to—by using your **systems, policies,** and **standard operating procedures**.

Through this book, you've learned how to be a great marketer and a great strategist. Unfortunately, you've probably taught yourself to be the *worst* leader possible because you're the doer, not the delegator.

Enter a brand new skill set—getting clarity on your desired business outcomes, then communicating them to your team so often and with such clarity, that they *get it*. Leadership means becoming a great coach as opposed to a great marketer. Those two things are fundamentally different.

The premise behind the book *Multipliers* is that some leaders multiply people while other leaders diminish people. The difference is incredibly subtle. Entrepreneurs who are technically savvy are often diminishers without realizing it. Diminishers are usually more technically capable than the people who work for them. As a result, they're too hands-on. They do all the work. They *try* to tell people how to do it, but if it doesn't get done their way, they criticize the employee and re-do it themselves.

A multiplier is a person who seeks challenge. They create room for people to figure out how to do the work and become better at it than they ever were. If you've got ninja skills at something, your risk of being a diminisher is pretty high.

Becoming a multiplier is contrary to human nature because you're so damn good at what you do. If you try to teach another person how to write copy, and you look at the way they write, you think, *This is terrible.* Then you jump in there with, "Please, just do this differently." And the instant that happens, they get taught not to think, but to follow instructions.

In certain instances, your team needs to follow a system step by step. But in many instances, you want your people to think for themselves. You still achieve your outcome of getting better quality work, but you do it by asking them questions. Facilitate self-reflection. Set a challenge and create space for people to learn and figure things out for themselves.

"How do you think that could be improved? If world class is *here*, and novice is *there*, how would you rate this piece of work? How would you move it up the ladder?"

Alex Schoffen talks about a concept called lateral pressure. Most wannabe leaders use forward pressure on their teams—they *push*. "Move faster. We've got to get this goal achieved. Let's do it."

Everything takes effort. But lateral pressure means you help people define *their* outcomes. Help your team understand their outcomes, and then help them figure out what they need to accomplish to achieve those bigger and better ones. But facilitate, don't push. I'm not the guy pushing my team, I'm asking them, "What's important in our business for you to really shine? What's your big outcome that's going to help this business, and how can I help you achieve it?"

Let's say you've got an operations manager whose deliverable this coming quarter is an updated Digital Agency Operations Manual. Say to them, "What does it mean to you to create a great operations manual? And how do we measure that it's been done?"

Now they start thinking, *Maybe I can create a folder structure for all the documents to go into. I can identify the ten most crucial functions in our business and start there.*

Then take their answer and turn it into specific deliverables. Now my question is, "We've got a twelve-week cycle ahead of us. What happens week by week to move that forward? How do you know that you're on track? How does the rest of the team know that you're on track?"

Now my operations manager owns the result. I no longer do, so I don't have to push. I've created lateral pressure with OKRs—**Objectives and Key Results**. Most Silicon Valley companies use OKRs.

Every Monday, from 11:30 to 1:00, we have a team meeting. And during that meeting we discuss various things. We talk about how we're doing with our quarterly objectives, what issues need to be resolved, and we give shoutouts to people who are doing great work. Facilitate good team communication, and you'll always know exactly what areas you need to work on.

Another tool I use is a daily team huddle. A daily team huddle is fifteen minutes, same time every day. What's in the cards for today? What decisions do we need to make? Who needs a little support? Who caught someone else doing something right? People live for that. That's why they show up. People leave people, not companies. And the reason why they leave people is they don't get the recognition they work so hard for.

Schedule a quarterly planning session where you review the previous quarter. Ask, "What are our big outcomes for the next quarter?" And define the crap out of your OKRs so it's absolutely clear to everybody what your priorities are.

"As an employee, how do I contribute towards that goal? How do I know I'm on track? How does everybody else know I'm on track?"

This structure facilitates peak performance, even with mediocre people on your team. Leading your team right is crucial. Otherwise, you hire two or three people, then two or three months into it, you get burnt out, and it's just easier to do it yourself again. And it's cheaper. Then you hire another two people, burn out again, and repeat the cycle. That doesn't work long-term.

But if you do that well for a year and a half, two years maybe, then you can leave. My family and I just returned from a three weeks vacation in the Mediterranean. And you know what? There wasn't one thing in my business that broke. There were no crises. The business actually grew. My team became better. Their communication was fantastic with one another. So now that allows me to go spend three weeks in Thailand, a month in the United States, and take a cruise in the Caribbean. All of that's possible because of my systems. I'm not that necessary to the operations anymore.

It's an ongoing process to extricate yourself from certain functions in your business, but as soon as you define your operations, build a team to take over your duties. *That* is the sexiest business on the planet to buy.

At this point, maybe you decide to sell. Or you start taking on other kinds of work as well, like video production. That's a personal thing, depending on your own vision, and what types of work you like doing. If you're going to stick to leading an agency, and you want to grow it consistently, you'll still need a team.

Three months after graduating, some of our Agency FastTrack graduates have seven clients and are already starting to hire people because they're drowning in work. But it all starts with the skills. If you're really good at delivering results, you'll find a lot of clients really fast, and you'll build your team fairly rapidly.

Maybe that isn't your ambition. Maybe you just want to earn some extra cash. Maybe you're a mom who wants to spend more time with the kids. So you only have to have a couple of clients who each pay you $1,500 per month. In that case, it might be two or three years before you hire another person. It's all governed by your vision. What are you trying to accomplish in terms of growth at your own agency?

I'll never forget what bestselling author of the business systems classic T*he E-Myth: Why Most Businesses Don't Work and What to Do About It*, Michael Gerber, told me. "The purpose of a business is to give its owner more of a life."

If you're an empire builder who wants to drive fast sports cars and travel the world in luxury, that's exactly what you'll be able to do, culminating in a huge sale of your agency to a firm like Omnicom Group in

New York City or WPP in London. These multinational publicly traded corporations grow through acquisition—finding and buying scalable, sustainable digital agencies like yours.

Then again, maybe you want to homeschool your kids while providing financial stability for the entire family. Even two or three retainer clients with the occasional website outsourcing project thrown in produces a fantastic income.

For newlyweds who want to travel for a few years before kids come along, a digital agency offers a lock up and go lifestyle. Or maybe you want to spend more of your waking hours volunteering at a charity, like an animal shelter. Onboard a few retainer clients, manage freelancers on the additional projects they offer, and you're making the big bucks with very little work.

Your vision for your business must be based on your vision for you. Maybe you want to create wealth and sell your agency for a fortune; then focus on transitioning from lead generation specialist to project manager. Maybe you just want to have a few really cool clients; then find two or three freelancers you can call on for additional projects.

At this point in the book, you have all the knowledge you need. Your future is limited only by your imagination. Once you know what you want your digital agency to look like, you've got to follow the right path to acquire the accompanying skills in the fastest time possible.

So, what's your vision?

CHAPTER 12

WHAT'S NEXT? TAKE A.C.T.ION.

I believe that digital agencies are the best businesses in the world to build—if you follow the right path to start, build, and scale them. Follow the wrong path, and you'll absolutely *hate* this business. Jump in without a plan, and the only business worse than a digital agency is hospitality. Or maybe prostitution.

I wrote this book to serve as your road map to the *right* path, so that you're prepared for the journey you're about to begin. I wrote this book to show you not only *how* to start an agency—but just as importantly, if you *should*.

The laptop lifestyle *is* possible if you follow the right path. But I promise no wealth without work. I have no secret magic formula. Instead, I'm giving you a realistic view of a hot new business opportunity. If you're interested in running an agency, you need to know what the journey looks like. This book provides you with insight into the skills you need. But it's beyond the scope of this book to actually *give* you those skills. For that matter, *no* book can teach you a skill.

Right now, chances are you're thinking, *I love the idea of building an agency. I know I've got to build my agency correctly. So once I put down this book, what's next? Where do I go from here?*

At this point, a lot of people rush off to get clients, or get Google PPC certified.

They think, *I can wing it. I'm on Instagram all the time. I feel proficient with Facebook. I like Tweeting. How hard could it be? Let's get paying clients first. Then I'll figure it out.*

Wrong. Anyone who thinks like that doesn't deserve to get paid. They rip off their clients, and they won't keep them for long.

Then we have the entrepreneurs. They think, *I'm going to get business because I've got the skills. All I do is get trained and certified, and businesses will know they can trust me with their marketing.*

Nope. Wrong again. Technical proficiency doesn't guarantee clients. Client acquisition is *itself* a skill set. It's no wonder so many agencies struggle and starve. Their owners have the skills to get their *clients* clients. But they don't know how to find, vet, and close their *own* clients. It's crazy.

In fact, *everything* I talk about in this book is a unique skill. Running Facebook ad campaigns. Building Funnels. Reaching the double-digit client mark. Hiring freelancers and managing projects. Finding full-time employees who match your values. Unless you go into this with previous business ownership experience, you're a virgin. And there's no shame there.

Unlike these gurus who promise overnight success and instant riches, I want you to be able to create a better future. Not just dream about one. You want more time, more money, and more freedom. Yet most entrepreneurs never get there. They read a book like this one, feel inspired, and do what comes naturally—which is almost always the wrong next step.

Take a business in a different niche. Let's say you have a cousin who loves animals. She loves grooming her dogs and helping her fellow dog owners at the park. So she starts a poodle clipping salon.

I get to work with animals all day long! she thinks. *This is fantastic! I love poodles.*

What did your cousin miss here? She didn't realize marketing is required to get the freaking animals through the door in the first place. She has to hire and manage staff. She has to master bookkeeping and accounting. Her business is not *just* about the animals. In fact, your cousin works directly with animals maybe five percent of her entire day.

CHAPTER 12 - WHAT'S NEXT? TAKE A.C.T.ION.

The point is, most people who start companies are so ill-informed, they end up awfully disappointed once the thing is up and running. Yes, you need to know your outcome when you start. You need to know why you're doing this in the first place—selling your digital agency for a pretty penny, for example. Whatever success looks like for you, it's going to be hard to get there. Starting a business is very difficult. That's guaranteed. But I *promise* you—you won't mind the hardships if you arrive at your destination.

While the previous chapter helped you understand your destination, I now want to help you find the best way to get *there*—you cashing out several years from now—from *here*—you reading this book right now.

I've taken everything I know about growing a digital agency from startup to sale and turned it into a three-stage journey called **The A.C.T. Model™**. Ask any successful agency entrepreneur or owner, and they'll tell you they follow these same steps, in this same order.

So, what are they?

The first digital agency stage is **Apprenticeship**. You enter this phase with knowledge and end this phase with knowledge *and* skills. In this business, you can't acquire skills until you have clients because no free (or paid) tutorial imparts skills. And you can't bill people for those skills until you've got them.

Why? Because skills from new client acquisition to high ROI campaign management cannot be learned by reading a book. Only when you schedule a live call with a prospect and run a campaign can you really nail these skills. So, the problem is, where do you get these clients and these campaigns before you *have* clients and campaigns?

Apprenticeship is the answer. There are two ways you can get an apprenticeship. First, you could work for an established digital agency. Your supervisor teaches you some (but not all) of the profitable skills you need to start your own business. But the chances that you'll *learn* all of the skills are very slim. That's just not how it works. If you start with little to no agency experience, you'll get paid peanuts and get assigned all the crappy work no one else wants to do. Not recommended.

Your other option is to work under the tutelage and guidance of people who are invested in your success. These mentors will not only *teach* you the skills, they'll help you *improve* your skills in real-time as you practice. Here's what I love about mentors—*they've gone where you want to go.* They guide you like a Sherpa. When people climb Mount Kilimanjaro for the first time, they never, *ever* do it alone. Not one aspiring mountaineer will even consider climbing solo on their first ascent. Because it's a one-way ticket. Literally suicide. Climb that mountain on your own, and you're not coming back.

Running a business is harder. It's a mountain that grows taller the higher you climb. Why would you require a Sherpa to take you up to Mount Kilimanjaro, but not a mentor to teach you business skills? If you're serious about digital agency success, your best bet is to get a Sherpa, a guide, a mentor who has walked the path. They can shine a torch and say to you, "Step here, not there. Learn this, not that."

I don't care who you do an apprenticeship with as long as you do one. But don't launch an agency until you know what you're doing, and until you've got the skills to produce ROI.

The second stage of The A.C.T. Model™ is **Clients**.

It doesn't matter how good you are with people. It doesn't matter how good you are at relationship-building. It doesn't matter if you mean well. It doesn't matter if you're a hard worker. It doesn't matter if you deserve success.

Only two things matters in this business—your ability to get clients, and your ability to produce results for them.

Just as getting an apprenticeship to *learn* is a distinct stage, so is finding and serving your first paying clients. This book gives you the knowledge, but only real life can give you the skills.

Remember, you can't start with clients. Apprenticeship comes first. When you've completed your apprenticeship, then it's time to get clients. At this stage, nothing else matters. Get clients, produce results, get more clients, produce more results.

The smartest way to build your clientele is follow everything in this book. Choose a niche. Hustle your ass off. Get your first two or three clients.

Rendering a good quality service matters, and your clients' ROI alone will generate referrals. They won't be able to shut up about you!

CHAPTER 12 - WHAT'S NEXT? TAKE A.C.T.ION.

Sometimes the phone rings off the hook for months at a time, and you can't take on all the work. Then, out of a nowhere, you hit a dry spell.

Word-of-mouth alone isn't sustainable, predictable, or scalable. That's why you can't take client acquisition skills for granted. You have no business hiring freelancers or building a full-time team to replace you until your marketing system works without you, scheduling so many appointments with buck prospects that you have to stop taking on clients.

The only agencies that survive are the ones with a business development system in place. Period. Make your growth predictable, then grow your agency. Only then have you truly completed the Clients stage.

On to the third digital agency stage, **Transcendence**. When you begin this stage, you're thinking, *I am skilled. I am the person who produces results.* When you end this stage—whatever that looks like for you—you're thinking, *My team produces the results, not me.*

Everything you learned in Chapter 11 allows you to transcend your business. You build your agency to succeed far beyond you. It's a radically different skillset. Transcendence is paradoxical—you go from the best technician in the world to the worst technician on your team. You've hired and trained subject matter experts who can run circles around you. *And that's the way it should be.* The only reason to start, build, and scale an agency is Transcendence. Get the skills, teach the skills, and get yourself out of the business.

Talk to anybody running a seven-figure digital agency, and they will confirm—The A.C.T. Model™ is the *only* path to achieve your agency dreams. And right now, the *only* path to complete the Apprenticeship, Clients, and Transcendence stages in four months (or less) is **Agency FastTrack**, the program you've seen referenced throughout this book.

Before I go any further, I want to level with you. Reading a book is a lot easier than going through a program like this. On average, only thirteen percent of people finish courses they join.[1] Because they get sidetracked. They get shiny object syndrome. They buy the next course. They get stuck.

The trick to helping people succeed at running an agency is a different paradigm. It's not about buying a course. It's about learning the skills. To design Agency FastTrack, we completed an exhaustive study of what it takes to teach people the critical skills of starting, building, and scaling digital agencies. That's why Agency FastTrack is by far the most comprehensive course on the planet. But that's not why we have an insane ninety-two percent completion rate.

Agency FastTrack works because we've built in support structures and systems that motivate students to learn the skills, practice their skills, and test their skills on real paying clients. We do live training programs. Each student gets a one-on-one coach who has already completed the program and launched a successful agency. This coach does whatever it takes to keep you on the right path. Some weeks, it's kicking your ass. Some weeks, it's supporting you. Some weeks, it's helping you to understand how to utilize your time better.

To have any level of integrity in this world, I believe that if you promise someone, "I'm going to be your guide and help you run a business," you keep that promise. And because we make that promise in Agency FastTrack, it's *our* responsibility to figure out what you need to succeed.

Think about "normal" coaching. Some new guru shows up and says, "I can show you the way to the laptop lifestyle. Follow me!" You put all of your trust and faith in that coach. Then what happens? The coach provides you with some information, then you go and try to implement it. But you get stuck. So you quit.

"What happened? I told you to go and implement it," the guru says.

"Yeah, but I'm having difficulty," you say.

"Then you must not want success badly enough."

No good coach says this. Work with the get-rich-quick schemers, and at every turn, your progress is solely your responsibility. You already know the perils of free online tutorials—if they actually helped, why would they be free?—and you know why most courses aren't worth their weight in elephant dung. You might "get" the concepts, but you battle to make them work.

CHAPTER 12 - WHAT'S NEXT? TAKE A.C.T.ION.

Most coaches only care about consistent sales, not student success rates. You bought information you already know, yet have no more ROI-producing skills than when you started. Don't subsidize fools who promise the world. If overnight success was possible, why would you need to buy a $997 Facebook advertising guide, a $2,400 copywriting course, and a $4,000 online business launch program?

You're also on the hook for all the software those coaches tell you to buy, from video production software to website plugins. Even a novice will figure out how they work, but using them to turn a hundred bucks into three hundred requires a skill set you just can't get in a tutorial or plugin. Not recommended!

Good coaches know the problem isn't the information or the technology alone. The biggest problem is implementation—and everything that gets in the way. Some people don't have enough drive. Some people have psychological issues and self-sabotage themselves. Some people are just no good at follow through. Some people suffer from shiny object syndrome.

When I created the first syllabus for Agency FastTrack, I made it very clear to my team—*We will not give ourselves excuses for our students' failures.* If our students fail, it's because of us, not because of them.

If you're serious about this, and you invest with us, *you will graduate.* In the most recent Agency FastTrack group, we had two students who had a death in the family. One student lost her sister suddenly, and another lost her husband. Another student had a baby ten weeks into the program. Four more students traveled internationally for weeks at a time. *All of them completed the program.*

And all of them are now the proud owners of profitable digital agencies. My point is, getting people started is the easy part. Getting them to finish is the hard part. But we're damn successful at both.

Agency FastTrack pairs coaching with technical support. No other program provides technical support. Why do we do this? Because that's where people get stuck. Who comes out of the womb knowing how to build a Funnel? Nobody! We not only teach you, we *help* you. So if you get stuck, we physically solve your problem. If you get stuck on an ad campaign, an Agency FastTrack graduate works with you directly on your own campaigns to increase conversions.

I refuse to measure the success of Agency FastTrack on courses sold or profit made. Your success in starting, building, and scaling a profitable agency is our one and only benchmark.

If you can see running a digital agency in your future, you owe it to yourself to get the best mentorship, guidance, and support you possibly can to maximize your chances of success.

Because failing in business is not fun. It's excusable, but it's not fun. Failure sets you back psychologically and financially in ways you cannot predict. So prevent failure from the start. Invest that extra bit of cash into the tried and proven A.C.T. Model™—and into an organization that cares about student success above all.

If you're ready for the next step, go to FreeAgencyBook.com/ThankYou. You'll complete a short form and schedule a breakthrough session with an Agency FastTrack strategist. You will *not* speak with a hardcore closer who gets paid twenty percent commission. Our job is to see if you really are ready for the digital agency opportunity. From there, both parties will discern if we're a good fit for one another.

If you've opted in at TheACTModel.com or through the bonuses provided in this book, you'll already receive free tools straight from Agency FastTrack. You'll get to understand our culture and our ethos. And you'll also be able to see if you're a good fit for the program.

But if you're ready to pull the trigger right now, talk to my team. We don't accept all students—only the right ones. Is that you? Go to FreeAgencyBook.com/ThankYou to find out. Have a look at the road ahead of you.

CHAPTER 12 - WHAT'S NEXT? TAKE A.C.T.ION.

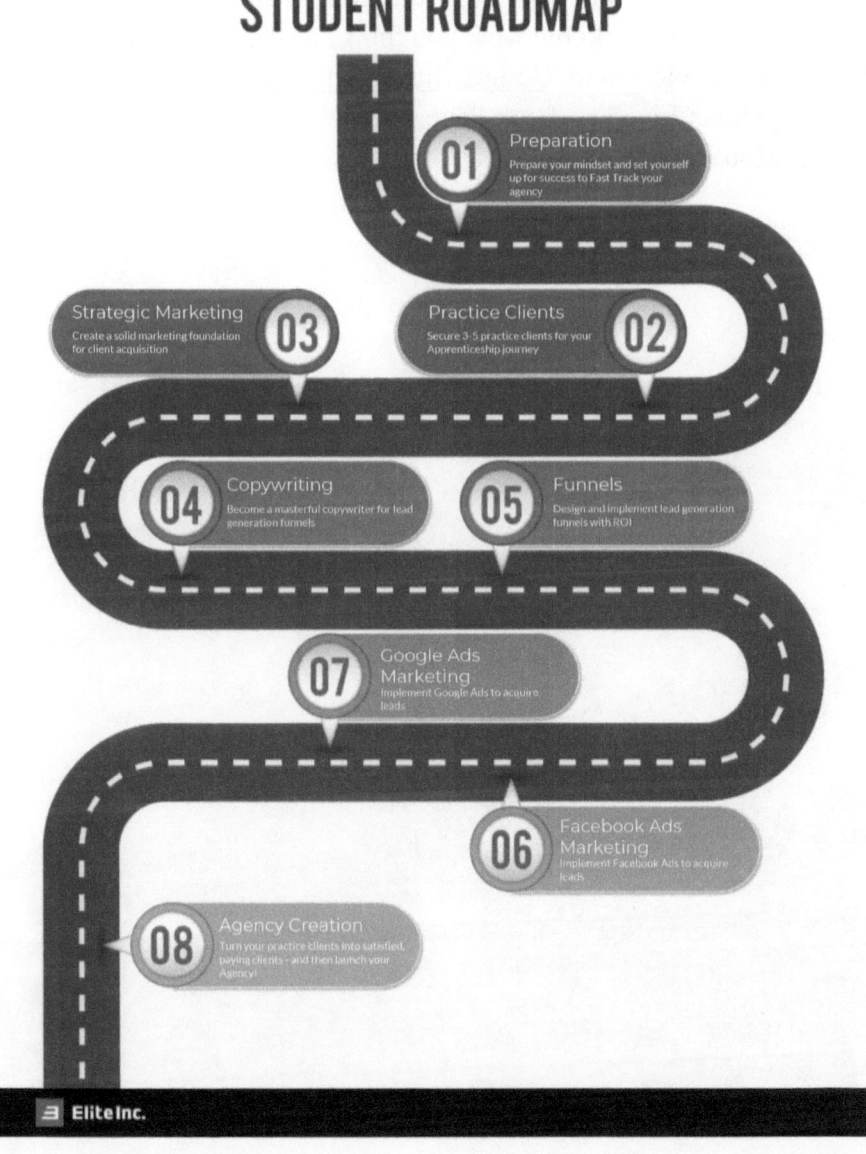

Whatever tools you choose to help you start, build, and scale your digital agency, remember—take things one step at a time. Refer to this book often to make sure you're still on the right path. Do that, and your business is practically foolproof.

Now, there's no time to waste. Your dreams are waiting.

Want to let others know what you think? Make your opinion known by leaving a review here: [Google Business Listing](#)

[Niel Malan Live Facebook Page](#)

Amazon Review

NOTES

Chapter 1

1. Rashid, Brian. "The Rise Of The Freelancer Economy." Forbes. January 26, 2016. Accessed July 4, 2018. https://www.forbes.com/sites/brianrashid/2016/01/26/the-rise-of-the-freelancer-economy/#1cc7bbad3bdf.
2. "Wayne Gretsky Quotes." BrainyQuote. Accessed July 5, 2018. https://www.brainyquote.com/quotes/wayne_gretzky_383282.
3. William, David. "70 Percent of Small Businesses Plan to Increase Digital Marketing Spend." Small Business Trends. January 23, 2017. Accessed July 5, 2018. https://smallbiztrends.com/2017/01/digital-marketing-spend-in-2017.html.
4. Moorman, Christine. "CMO Survey Report: Highlights and Insights." The CMO Survey. August 2016. Accessed July 5, 2018. https://cmosurvey.org/wp-content/uploads/sites/11/2016/08/The_CMO_Survey-Highlights_and_Insights-Aug-2016.pdf.
5. Slefo, George. "Acquisitions Of Digital Agencies, Ad-Tech and Analytics Firms Surge." Ad Age. August 10, 2016. Accessed July 5, 2018. http://adage.com/article/agency-news/digital-properties-dominated-mergers-acquisitions/305397/
6. Rafatali. "How Much Is That Digital Media Company Really Worth? A Guide." Poynter. April 10, 2017. Accessed July 5, 2018. https://www.poynter.org/news/how-much-digital-media-company-really-worth-guide.

Chapter 2

1. Vomiero, Jessica. "Facebook Has Lost $100B in Value — and Its Money Problems May Just Be Beginning." Global

News. March 27, 2018. Accessed July 5, 2018. https://globalnews.ca/news/4108493/facebook-money-problems/.
2. Monk, Chris. "Facebook Has Stopped Messenger Bots – Here's What You Need to Know." Mumbrella. April 6, 2018. Accessed July 5, 2018. https://mumbrella.com.au/facebook-has-stopped-messenger-bots-heres-what-you-need-to-know-509654.
3. France, Sue. "The Fixed Mindset vs. The Growth Mindset." American Society of Administrative Professionals. Accessed July 5, 2018. https://www.asaporg.com/all-articles/fixed-mindset-vs-growth-mindset.

Chapter 3

1. Cunningham, Steve. "Seth Godin on What It Takes to Be a Linchpin [INTERVIEW]." Mashable. February 14, 2010. Accessed July 5, 2018. https://mashable.com/2010/02/14/seth-godin-linchpin/#l8VqqWP4Fqqu.
2. "Linchpin." Dictionary.com. Accessed July 5, 2018. http://www.dictionary.com/browse/linchpin.
3. Koch, Richard. "The 80/20 Principle : The Secret of Achieving More With Less." March 1998. Accessed July 5, 2018. http://www.portalalfa.com/time/books/book1.htm.
4. Staff, Inc. "The Simple Way Michael Dubin Came Up With Dollar Shave Club." Inc. December 22, 2017. Accessed July 5, 2018. https://www.inc.com/video/michael-dubin/how-michael-dubin-came-up-with-his-breakthrough-idea-for-dollar-shave-club.html.
5. Primack, Dan. "Unilever Buys Dollar Shave Club for $1 Billion." Fortune. July 20, 2016. Accessed July 5, 2018. http://fortune.com/2016/07/19/unilever-buys-dollar-shave-club-for-1-billion/.

Chapter 4

1. LaMorte, Wayne W., MD, PhD, MPH. "Diffusion of Innovation Theory." Behavioral Change Models. April 28, 2016. Accessed July 5, 2018. http://sphweb.bumc.bu.edu/otlt/

MPH-Modules/SB/BehavioralChangeTheories/Behavioral-ChangeTheories4.html.
2. Blogger, CHI. "The Art of Attracting New Buyers." Chet Holmes International. September 4, 2013. Accessed July 5, 2018. https://blog-chetholmes.com/2013/09/04/attracting-new-buyers/.
3. "Rule of 7: How Social Media Crushes Old School Marketing." Kruse Control Inc. March 29, 2018. Accessed July 5, 2018. https://www.krusecontrolinc.com/rule-of-7-how-social-media-crushes-old-school-marketing/.

Chapter 5

1. Chopra, Paras. "Lessons Learned from 21 Case Studies in Conversion Rate Optimization." Moz. August 3, 2010. Accessed November 5, 2018. https://moz.com/blog/lessons-learned-from-21-case-studies-in-conversion-rate-optimization-10585.
2. Patel, Niel. "10 Ways To Create High Converting Headlines." QuickSprout. April 25, 2013. Accessed November 5, 2018. https://www.quicksprout.com/2013/04/25/10-ways-to-create-high-converting-headlines/.
3. Hangen, Nathan. "David Ogilvy's 7 Tips for Writing Copy That Sells." Neil Patel. Accessed July 5, 2018. https://neilpatel.com/blog/david-ogilvy/.
4. Rayson, Steve. "We Analyzed 100 Million Headlines. Here's What We Learned (New Research)." Buzzsumo. June 26, 2017. Accessed July 5, 2018. http://buzzsumo.com/blog/most-shared-headlines-study/#gs.XyfZ4K8.
5. Rayson, 2017.
6. Petrovick, Terry. "Jay Abraham on Amazon Copy Writing Secrets." YouTube. April 14, 2011. Accessed July 5, 2018. https://www.youtube.com/watch?v=7GISK7aZkpk.
7. "Jay Abraham on Copywriting." Abraham. Accessed July 5, 2018. https://www.abraham.com/jayoncopywriting/.
8. Wood, Kristan. "Gin Experiences in the Cape." What's

on in Cape Town. May 31, 2018. Accessed December 04, 2018. https://www.whatsonincapetown.com/post/gin-experiences-cape/.
9. Patel, Sahil. "85 Percent of Facebook Video Is Watched without Sound." Digiday. May 17, 2016. Accessed July 5, 2018. https://digiday.com/media/silent-world-facebook-video/.

Chapter 6

1. Kim, Larry. "7 Conversion Rate Truths That Will Change Your Landing Page Strategy." Search Engine Land. April 15, 2014. Accessed July 5, 2018. https://searchengineland.com/7-conversion-rate-truths-will-change-landing-page-optimization-strategy-191083.

Chapter 9

1. Lahkiani, Vishen. "Risk Reversal: My Favorite Jay Abraham Technique For Kick-Starting Your Online Sales (Insight #3)." Mindvalley Insights. May 9, 2012. Accessed July 5, 2018. http://www.mindvalleyinsights.com/risk-reversal-jay-abraham-technique/.

Chapter 11

1. "Online Business Tools." Brad Sugars Profit Masters. Accessed January 03, 2019. http://bradsugarsprofitmasters.com/online-business-tools-content/.

Chapter 12

1. Ruocco, Carolyn. "Why Can't I Find Stats on Elearning Completion Rates?" Medium. June 14, 2017. Accessed July 5, 2018. https://medium.com/no-way-out-but-forward/why-cant-i-find-stats-on-elearning-completion-rates-b86ee3edf053.

www.ingramcontent.com/pod-product-compliance
Lightning Source LLC
Chambersburg PA
CBHW030647220526
45463CB00005B/1663